STEPHEN T. BERG

The story of Edmonton's Hope Mission

GROWING HOPE

Belleville, Ontario, Canada

Growing Hope

Copyright © 2010, Stephen T. Berg

ISBN: 978-1-55452-450-1

To order additional copies, visit:
www.essencebookstore.com

For more information, please contact:
Stephen T. Berg
780.422.2018
stephen.berg@hopemission.com
www.hopemission.com
or
stephen@stephentberg.com

Guardian Books is an imprint of *Essence Publishing,* a Christian Book Publisher dedicated to furthering the work of Christ through the written word. For more information, contact:
20 Hanna Court, Belleville, Ontario, Canada K8P 5J2
Phone: 1-800-238-6376 • Fax: (613) 962-3055
E-mail: info@essence-publishing.com
Web site: www.essence-publishing.com

November 24, 2009

Hope is an unusual thing...at times strong and unshakable, at others fragile and fleeting. From its creation in 1929, the Hope Mission has served as an invaluable lifeline for people in our community who have lost all hope or are struggling to hang on to their dreams for the future. For some, hope has been delivered in the form of a hot meal and a warm, safe place to spend the night. Others have found hope in programs the Mission offers to those fleeing abuse and battling addiction or to youth who are seeking a more positive direction for the future. Over the past 80 years, countless people have seen their hope rekindled and strengthened thanks to the care, compassion and understanding offered by Mission staff and volunteers.

As Her Majesty the Queen's representative in Alberta, it's my pleasure to offer sincere thanks to everyone who played a role in helping the Hope Mission reach this impressive milestone. I'd also like to offer best wishes for continued success in the years to come. As long as there is a need, may you continue to grow hope and faith in the hearts of the most vulnerable people among us.

Sincerely yours,
Norman L. Kwong, CM AOE
Lieutenant Governor of Alberta

MAYOR STEPHEN MANDEL
CITY OF EDMONTON

October 28, 2009

Mr. Stephen Berg

Dear Mr. Berg,

Thank you for the opportunity to provide words in support of Hope Mission's recently completed book, a compilation of its history entitled "Growing Hope, the Story of Edmonton's Hope Mission—the First 80 Years. I would like to express my sincerest congratulations on this achievement.

Hope Mission continues to be a centre of welcoming, serving and caring for those in our community that are in need. Sharing Hope Mission's 80 year history is a way to recognize its importance to our city and inspire hope for the future of the organization and those it serves.

I am pleased to congratulate you once again.

Yours truly,
Stephen Mandel
Mayor

Contents

Foreword

In 1928, optimism was sky high. Credit was free. Herbert Hoover, the highly regarded president of the United States, said that the USA would never know poverty again. We now know that this was an immense misreading. Overnight, the markets and the economy failed. The debacle of that failure was properly called a crash, and it involved the whole world. No one was prepared for the fallout, certainly not governments. In the summer of 1929, trains crossed the country with hundreds of men riding on top of boxcars, going anywhere just to find a job.

Edmonton wasn't spared. In the midst of this situation, the Edwardsons acquired an old cauldron. In an act of Christian charity, Mrs. Edwardson gathered outdated vegetables and transformed them into good soup and began to serve the hungry. A new term was born: *soup kitchen*. This was the beginning. It was simple and sparse, but men were being cared for.

It's a privilege to write this brief introduction, because I have long had a heart for Hope Mission. From my first visit in 1935, shortly after I was saved, I felt a sense of belonging. The Mission, as a place to serve my Lord, seemed to fit with me. I didn't have to make it fit. To serve God at Hope Mission for over sixty years, with the support of my family, has been a privilege and a joy, never drudgery. For this I am ever thankful to God.

I hope you enjoy reading and learning about the history of Hope Mission and how God has provided for it, all the while using it to reach out to those in need.

May the name of Jesus Christ always be honoured at Hope Mission.

This foreword was written by Herb Jamieson (1912–2003) at the request of the author, in anticipation of the publication of Hope Mission's history.

Acknowledgements

Thanks to all staff, former staff and volunteers past and present who made the story worth telling and who provided information whenever possible. A special thanks to Herb Jamieson, Dagmar Cunningham, Lilly Lewis, Harold Burma, Ed Enarson and Bruce Reith for your willingness to share any and all remembrances.

A very special thank you to Cheryl Kaye Tardif, for willingly applying her editing expertise to the entire manuscript. Cheryl, author of the popular novel *Whale Song*, has a special connection to Hope Mission. Her brother, Jason Kaye, used the services of Hope Mission before he was murdered in 2006.

As well, my heartfelt thanks to Mary Sullivan, author and teacher, for her unfailing encouragement. Finally, a bouquet of unreserved gratitude to my wife, Debbie, for keeping me on track and on task and doing so with loving charity.

Preface

Growing Hope is quite simply a story of God's providential care. The story takes place in Edmonton but could just as well have taken place wherever faithful people come together in response to God's personal call to care for those in need. Therefore, while this is an account of the life of Hope Mission, it is more properly a tribute to the God of Jesus Christ who deeply loves the poor and oppressed, and calls willing hearts to compassion and care. In this way God's indiscriminate love becomes action that touches souls, brings reconciliation and transforms lives. It is all of these lives that this book hopes to honour.

In too many ways this is an incomplete accounting. An attempt was made to contact the leaders and other key people of the Mission and ask for their stories and experiences. This was only partially successful. Some have passed on, and others could not be located. Those we did manage to track down were gracious and free with what they remembered. To them, we extend our sincerest gratitude. An effort was also made to gather all archival records of Hope Mission. While that effort yielded some success, it soon became obvious that Hope Mission has always been more concerned with serving and forgetting what was behind and pressing on (Philippians 3:13-14) rather than documenting that service. There is something commendable about this approach; however, the reader will understand that this combination of action orientation and humility made the writing of Hope Mission's history more difficult. For that same reason many stories will remain untold and too many people who were part of that history will remain anonymous.

As every Hope Mission leader would tell you, the involvement of board members, staff and volunteers is inestimable in terms of the ongoing ministry of Hope Mission. So while this short history primarily recounts the stories and actions of the supervisors, directors, leaders and other key volunteers of the Mission, it is to busy board members and those on the front lines and in the *trenches* that this story is dedicated. To the scores of other Mission workers and volunteers who aren't mentioned, please know that the stories included here are a testament to your service. To those who have faithfully supported and prayed for this ministry over the years, Hope Mission owes its deepest gratitude.

Although this work is obviously unfinished, the mission and ministry of Hope Mission is in a profound way complete by its very presence. This is because of God's habit of bringing to fruitful completion that which is started in faith, hope and love. Hope Mission's watchword continues to be *hope*. Hope has been birthed, has grown and *is* growing through the ongoing presence of Christ. Hope Mission has had the great honour and privilege of being part of the expression and extension of that hope in the lives of those served over the years.

The staff and board members, past and present, consider it an honour to share this story with you. It is our prayer that you will be encouraged as you hear about God's work through Hope Mission.

Born of a Zealous Hope Through Eyes of Faith

We have this hope, a sure and steadfast anchor of the soul (Hebrews 6:19).

REV. HAROLD AND HILDVIG (HILLIE) EDWARDSON: THE NEED IS THE CALL

Walking south on 102 Street, past the old A. MacDonald building, across a paved parking lot where the CNR trains used to run, then to 104 Avenue, you see the Bell office tower throwing its giant shadow over 10321-102 Street. There is no longer a marked address there, just an L-shaped extension of the high-rise. But in 1929, there was a modest storefront with enough space for a gospel service or for a dozen men to bunk down or a few dozen men to wait shoulder to shoulder for a bowl of soup. The place wasn't nearly adequate, but it was space nevertheless, and the people who opened the doors saw to it that most everyone who waited eventually got something to eat or a place to rest, along with a word of encouragement. Inadequate as it seemed, it held promise and hope against the hastening sweep of what would become known as the Great Depression.

In 1929, hope faded. Canadian companies, dependent on the export of raw materials and grain, closed; farmers went bankrupt, banks failed, unemployment soared, and the Depression took hold. The need was acute, and everywhere there was a sense of urgency. In Edmonton the unemployed arrived, hoping for work, any work.

In the late spring of 1929 Rev. Harold Ingvald Edwardson stood at the construction site of the Leland Hotel and within half an hour observed scores of men requesting work and being turned away. The scene haunted him, and the burden of those men stayed with him. This great need became his call.

PREPARATION

Before Harold Edwardson was able to truly empathize with others in their despair, he experienced his own transformation and his own preparation.

As a young seaman on the northern coast of Norway he was not unfamiliar with a desolate lifestyle. He'd seen his share of dissipation. So when Harold walked into a Salvation Army hall in that "Land of the Midnight Sun" and for the first time came face to face with the story of Jesus and the claims of the gospel, he responded without reservation. Within a few short seasons he immigrated to Canada and moved to Edmonton. Deeply affected by this touch on his life and what he understood as a calling, he started preparing for a life of service.

In Edmonton, Harold attended the old Beulah Mission on 98 Street. While increasing his scriptural understanding and gaining fluency in English, he also found good company there and made some lasting and important connections, not the least of which was meeting his wife, Hillie Suvan.

Following their wedding, the new couple was called to begin a church in Bergen, Alberta. From there they moved to pastor a Mennonite Brethren church in Alsask. It was during their tenure there that the Edwardsons began to re-evaluate and seriously consider a change of ministry.

Rev. Edwardson was deeply committed to and saw value in all Christian work, but he also had a streak of independence—a character trait he would share with many Hope Mission directors—that motivated him to leave a church that he now felt was limiting him and his ministry. Even more than this, the vision and desire to serve the neediest that began in a dimly lit Salvation Army hall across the ocean returned and took shape in a new way. In Harold's words, "God's call to [these] other avenues of service crystallized."

For Mrs. Edwardson, her experience of God's call was just as clear. Speaking about their decision to leave the pastorate after more than thirteen years, she stated with a simple directness that was her hallmark, "My husband and I were definitely called to a different line of work."

The Edwardsons arrived back in Edmonton in the spring of 1929. Full of expectation and ready to follow God's lead (believing that it may take them north to the territories), they prayed, waited and watched. In the meantime they rented a house downtown on 97 Street. To help with the rent they sublet some rooms.

There were obvious and deep needs right in the heart of Edmonton, and friends urged them to consider mission work. When Rev. Edwardson stood off to the side watching the plight of jobless and homeless men filing by the construction site of the Leland Hotel, his heart broke open, and the question of staying in Edmonton was settled.

Birth Pangs

After renewing friendships and re-establishing connections, the Edwardsons invited a few interested and supportive friends to form a board of directors. They now needed a hall. As Hillie Edwardson reported, "It was not an easy task. Rents still were up in price, and it was hard to find anything suitable." Besides this, most landlords didn't want to rent; they wanted to sell. An empty store was finally located on 10321—102 Street, and through the support of the first Hope Mission board, the Edwardsons arranged for a month's rent.

That first board included Mr. Royal Goodie, Mrs. Mary Finlay, Mrs. Clara Price and Marrion Hull as members. Every small gift from a concerned individual was truly appreciated, but the board knew that for the Mission to gain a foothold they would need increased and more consistent financial support.

The Edwardsons' daughter, Dagmar Cunningham, recalls that while she was helping to scrub, paint and generally refurbish the old storefront, two business men arrived to see what was happening. They spoke with her dad. She didn't hear the conversation, but the following day a cheque for $200 arrived. In Dagmar's words, "That was the seal!" The two men, Alfred Skenfield and J. F. Lymburn, were trustees of the Tegler Trust later the Tegler Foundation. The trust was created under the terms of Robert Tegler's will and was the first charitable trust established in Alberta. In the coming years the Tegler Trust would follow up that donation with many more, and, especially in these formative years, the trust would be the primary supporter of Hope Mission.

Hope Mission opened its doors on September 22, 1929, but by the spring of 1930 the Edwardsons and the board were looking for larger facilities. If there had been any misgivings about the need for this work and God's leading in starting Hope Mission, they were gone. The Mission held two services most evenings. Complementing whatever food they were able to share were hymns and a gospel message. In an early board report Mrs. Edwardson wrote, "Many were seeking Christ and finding a Saviour from sin." Even the theft of the Edwardsons' autoharp didn't dampen the enthusiasm of those early days.

The Edwardsons fed the men as best as they could. Mrs. Edwardson would boil as much porridge as available and allot a bowlful to each man until it ran out. Over the next few months they made a connection with Queen City Meats, and through the generosity of this business Hillie was able to make soup and occasionally even stew for the men. Word of the Mission spread, and soon hundreds of men flocked to the little storefront in search of a modicum of comfort and a bite to eat. There was little room for shelter, however, and only the dozen or so men who arrived first would get a safe and dry place to sleep. If there were two or three men who were sick or in some other way in greater need, they would be invited home by the Edwardsons for the night. Because of this burgeoning need and the ongoing operating expense, the Mission's immediate future was precarious. This weighed heavily on the heart of Harold Edwardson.

RUNNING ON FAITH

It's common knowledge that many missions' budgets are hand to mouth. The phrase *running on faith* has become idiomatic in describing this reality. Hope Mission, like many missions, was birthed and nurtured through faith. So for the Edwardsons, the fact that the Mission was presently broke did not so much beg the question of whether to go on but was instead an occasion for more prayer and perhaps discovering which new direction to take. On April 30, 1930, Harold Edwardson decided to find work to help carry the Mission. But on that day a $100 donation came in, and a few days later $200 came in. On May 5th the Tegler trustees met. Minutes of that meeting, as outlined in Tegler Trust's history, read as follows:

> Mr. and Mrs. Edwardson were already doing good social work in a small way in a little Mission on 102 Street. They, being able, devoted and conscientious in work of the type, it was thought that a larger and more comprehensive institution was warranted...if a suitable place could be found for the purpose, they [the Tegler Trust] would assist them financially.

By the middle of May arrangements were made for leasing the large CNR staff rooming house at 10521-101 Street. Hope Mission was gaining a reputation of doing good work among the unemployed and hungry men, and because of this CNR made the rooming house available to the Mission. On May 22, 1930, the Tegler Trust followed up with a $1,700 donation, in order, as their minutes state, "to buy the goodwill, fixtures and furnishings of the rooming house." Having been renovated from top to bottom, with a large meeting hall in the basement, a shoe repair shop, office and suites, the *new* Hope Mission opened on July 1, 1930.

In the fall of 1930, with the Depression strengthening its grip, there was talk on the street of food riots. The city implemented an emergency relief program to defuse the situation. Hope Mission was approached to look after the daily feeding of hundreds of men while the city would supply the food, which almost always consisted of porridge. The Edwardsons agreed to the arrangement for one year. A block away from the Mission, the old Immigration Hall, which had stood empty with its large kitchen, was now pressed into service. Many unemployed and destitute men from across the country came through Edmonton. The Immigration Hall was a place where they found enough food to stave off hunger, at least for a while. By one account, at the height of the Depression it was not uncommon for a man to line up for a bowl of porridge with over 1,000 men and then after eating go back to the end of the line. The men claimed that "By the time you reached the front again you'd be hungry, and there wasn't anything else to do anyway."

In the volume *Fury and Futility: The Onset of the Great Depression,* which is part of a journalistic history of Alberta published by United Western Communications Ltd., there is a telling account of Hope Mission's expanded work and its new political relationship with the city:

> In Edmonton, the lot of the single unemployed grew worse. The city could hardly let these men freeze and starve. It had hurriedly turned over the old Immigration Hall to the Hope Mission, which was run by the Rev. Harold Edwardson and his wife, to enlarge its operations. When close to 500 men paraded in Market Square, Mayor Douglas directed them to the Mission. About 150 took his advice. Crowded it unquestionably was, but when trade council member Carl Berg complained about it, the mayor and the Edwardsons defended themselves in the *Edmonton Journal.*
> "I tasted the [breakfast] porridge myself," Mayor Douglas assured the newspaper. "It was quite good. I know something about porridge too." Mrs. Edwardson said that Mr. Berg had never visited the hall, adding that there were no complaints when the Hope Mission was operating privately and it was only now, after the city had got involved, that agitators felt free to complain. Furthermore, the soup she served was thick and rich enough to jell when it was cold. "The last batch contained fifty pounds of shank beef, sixteen or seventeen pounds of split peas and fifteen pounds of onions," she said. As for keeping the hall clean, the men themselves did nothing. "Mostly," she said, "they pile off as soon as they are fed. They don't seem to do much cleaning up after themselves."

Although the arrangement with the city lasted only a year, it was not without some relief that the Edwardsons turned the Immigration Hall back to the city.

A GROWING IDENTITY

The early years saw the Mission quickly establish itself as a place of compassion. It was a place where every bowl of soup was ladled out with empathy. Nevertheless, the work was hard, often tedious, and although the Mission staff had grown to twelve by the mid-thirties, there was always more work.

The Edwardsons put in long days. Harold Edwardson, feeling the emotional strain of the ministry, often suffered severe headaches as well as with a digestive disorder. Dagmar said of her mother, "She worked very hard. She was often completely exhausted by the end of the day. But she was a strong woman and she always came through. She was outgoing and a real go-getter."

Hillie Edwardson's character and personality won her respect and endeared her to people. One of these was the manager of MacDonald's Consolidated, a grocery wholesale enterprise. His business was only a block away from the Mission, and he often came by to visit and to see how things were going. One day he came by and said, "Mrs. Edwardson, if you had your way, what would you like to do today?"

She quickly replied, "I'd like to give these men a meal of pork and beans—bread and coffee—all they can eat." To Hillie's sheer delight, he responded at once and set the machinery in motion. Hundreds of pounds of beans were provided, gallons of mustard and ketchup, and vats of coffee. Packing plants sent in bacon; bakeries donated bread in abundance. The Harmony White Lunch restaurant cooked beans in large drums all night and all the next day and then transported it to the hall by truck. Mrs. Edwardson, recalling the event in almost biblical terms, effused, "What a thrill it was to see 4,000 men have all they wanted to eat."

Walter Stevenson was one of the men caught in the grip of the Great Depression. In 1934, he set off with $30 in his pocket, earned from his work as a harvest field hand. Hoping to find work, he rode on top of box-cars across the prairies to Vancouver. Not finding work, running out of money and being ordered out of his rented room, he went back to the rail yard to catch a car to Edmonton. He was cold and wet when he arrived.

Walter explained, "Once back in Edmonton, I stood alone and cold on 101 Street. I walked until I came to a railway underpass and noticed a church-like building where it said Hope Mission. My only hope was that they would take me in. I knocked on the door to see if I could spend the night—it was so cold. To my joy and relief, the door opened and I was told that if I could find a corner somewhere I could stay. It was nice and warm the next morning. They were kind enough to give me a sandwich and a cup of warm milk—which I have never forgotten."

As the young Mission took shape, it was the Edwardsons' sustaining conviction that God's presence was continually evident in and through all these early encounters, events and circumstances. The times had called for practical care and compassion, and as these were given, Hope grew. All of the front-line work—the gathering and delivering, the feeding and repairing, the listening and counselling—every activity was couched in the prayer that men and women, young and old, would be affected by the love of Jesus Christ and give their lives to him. God answered this prayer regularly and consistently. As Rev. Harold Edwardson succinctly recorded: "Had great meetings, always full house. Many saved." Also, "A man in uniform has been restored to his earlier faith after years of backsliding." And again, "As a direct result of the Gospel Meetings of the Mission, we've had some very definite conversions of several young people."

Beyond the City

Although the Mission was located downtown and served the inner city, Hope Mission was unique in that it also extended itself into the rural areas. During the late thirties and into the early forties there was times where more aid was given in rural areas than in the city. The Depression hit the farming community hard. Adding to the collapse of the market was an almost unbearable drought lasting through most of the thirties. While thousands were forced to leave their farms, many tried to stay; those that did faced staggering hardship. When it was learned that Hope Mission was a place that could help, letters began arriving, requesting relief of any kind. In an effort to raise donations for these families in desperate need, Hope Mission would occasionally forward letters to the newspaper. One letter the *Edmonton Bulletin* published went like this:

> I heard that you have helped quite a few people. Will you please send some clothes for my wife and myself because we are in a bad condition for a year already. I will have to take my wife to the hospital for she is sick with so little to eat and wear. Our bed is made of boards with a mattress of hay covered with old sacks. We wish ourselves dead. If you don't believe how we suffer then I don't know what we will do. I got no underwear, no shoes, no socks, no shirts. My wife got no dresses. She wears overalls around the house. She has no shoes or a coat. Please do send us something. Please help us, oh, do help us.

Rev. Edwardson would occasionally go out to the country to visit some of the families that requested help from the Mission. One such visit was in the spring of 1942. Harold reported that he and the board chairman, Mr. Gleddie, visited a family that had come to their attention in February. "The situation was found to be most destitute, very little food; seven people living in a house in poor condition; two beds and one chair for the whole family." The Mission gave what they could and made sure the children had clothing.

Although initially rebuffed, the Mission was eventually able to get free freight carriage through strong appeals accompanied by first-hand accounts and excerpts of certain letters of desperation. Additionally, in what was Hope Mission's first direct mail campaign, the Edwardsons sent out hundreds of appeal letters.

People and businesses responded. Subsequently, the Mission set up a series of depots in the country and in this way was able to supply hundreds of rural families with shoes and clothing, some food, and other items as they became available.

Although by the early forties the need in the city was somewhat abated, there were still emergencies in the rural areas. Some people made the trip into Edmonton and to the doorstep of the Mission to ask for help in person or to offer something in exchange for needed items. Having saved $7, a mother with two young children made the trip to ask for shoes, clothing and coats for herself and her family in preparation for the coming winter. The clothes they had were badly worn and beyond repair. Upon her arrival she offered the $7 as a payment for whatever the Mission could help her with. She was sent on her way, not only with an adequate supply of serviceable clothing for her children, but also with a wonderful winter coat that fit her perfectly. When she got home and tried on the coat again, inside a side pocket she found her $7. Decades later, the woman's adult children came to the Mission to say what a lasting impression that act of true charity had made upon their family. They thanked Hope Mission again and left a generous donation for the ongoing work of the ministry.

Hope Mission gave where there was need, and the compassion of the Mission's leaders was in no way insular. In 1943, the presence of Hope Mission was even felt on the other side of the world. Hearing of the inhuman living conditions of Russian citizens, Hope Mission gathered, according to a board notation, "a considerable amount of supplies" and shipped them to

Russia. A newspaper report stated that the garments were valued at $1,680. At the same time, Hope Mission also became involved in an Edmonton-wide initiative called Clothing for Europe.

ROYAL RIBBONS

Life at the Mission wasn't always absorbed with the needs of ministry. There was often humour, even in the middle of calamity. Occasionally, life was even punctuated by imperial events. For a number of days in May 1939, Edmonton was caught up in a flurry of preparations for the first ever royal visit to Canada, including Edmonton. It was the social event of the decade. Hope Mission was brought into the regal fuss because King George VI and Queen Elizabeth would pass, in all their pomp, directly in front of the Mission on 101 Street.

In acknowledgement and preparation for this historic event, the minutes of the board meeting held May 18, 1939, read: "A motion by Mr. Williams, that Mr. Edwardson (Seconded Mr. Suder) be empowered to spend Five Dollars for decorations for the Royal Visit was passed." And so with expeditious Mission style, in preparation for an event of this nature, the better part of $5 was spent to buy four large ribbons, which were hung elegantly from the Mission's sign. Hope Mission, in its own inimitable way, was thus outfitted to honour the royal couple and, in turn, prepared to be graced by passing royal grandeur.

WOMEN OF HOPE

Women played a key role in the genesis, formation and evolution of Hope Mission. Early on, many of the women who contributed to the success of the ministry were wives of board members or supervisors. To say that these women were an integral part of the health and well-being of the Mission is to understate the case. They were part of the team, and in the formative years of the Mission they not only did much of the work; they were also key consultants and strategists. Without the support and in many cases direct and indirect leadership of these women, Hope Mission would never have been born. Not by accident were there more women than men on the board of directors that oversaw the birth of Hope Mission; and on subsequent boards of the early Mission, women always represented close to half of the board.

Mrs. Mary A. Finlay

Not all of the women who served the Mission were wives of Mission leaders. Mary Finlay was a charter member and an original founder of Hope Mission. She served on the board of directors from 1929 to 1959. Ron Gillespie, secretary at the time of Mary's resignation, wrote to her, "Words of appreciation can fall short of their objective, and after serving on the board for over thirty years we know that words are very inadequate in expressing our appreciation for your solid support and wise counsel."

Mary came to Edmonton in 1909 to help start the Beulah Mission, which was a shelter and a place of assistance for immigrant women and unwed mothers. In 1921, her husband of only three years died. Subsequently she took the position of superintendent of Beulah Home.

Mary was a close friend of Hillie (Suvan) Edwardson prior to Harold arriving on the scene, and their friendship had a musical result. While classmates at Beulah Bible School they discovered they each had a passion for singing and playing guitar. Their talent drew attention, and Hillie and Mary were invited to share their music in many churches throughout Alberta.

When the Edwardsons moved back to Edmonton they began attending the Beulah Mission Church. Mary and the Edwardsons quickly re-established their close friendship. They discovered in each other a common outlook and a common desire to care for the vulnerable, the poor and the hurting. As founder and supervisor of Beulah Home, Mary had practical experience and insight into the workings of a social care facility, and she shared her experience with the Edwardsons. It was the confident and energetic support of Mary Finlay that contributed to the founding of Hope Mission. After its launch, Mary although busy with her supervisory role at Beulah Home always took an active part in steering the young ministry.

Mary's heart was with people on the margins. In her forty-six-year role as Beulah Home supervisor, Mary cared for 5,300 single mothers and has been called the "foster mother of more than 3,800 babies." In 1962, the Junior Chamber of Commerce named Mary Finlay Edmonton's number-one citizen. Mayor Elmer Roper called her "a great and good citizen whose life and work have been an inspiration to all."

In the summer of 2000, Mary had an Edmonton park named in her honour, and a subsequent article in *The Edmonton Journal* (August 16, 2000) memorialized her with these words: "In the days when having a baby out of marriage brought unspeakable shame, Mary Finlay warmly welcomed the moms and their children to her home for unwed mothers." It was this kind of inspiration, compassion and dedication that Mary Finlay brought to the Mission.

DAGMAR CUNNINGHAM (EDWARDSON)

Born in Didsbury while her father was pastor at Bergen, Dagmar Edwardson arrived at the Mission when she was eight years old. She grew up in Hope Mission; her room was on the top floor of the Mission on 101 Street. At the age of ten she began playing piano for the Mission's services. She played six nights a week, and she also played for afternoon Sunday school. Dagmar recalled, "I got to know the *Old Redemption Hymnal* backwards and forwards. I can tell you today that number 200 is 'Jesus Saves' and number 78 is 'Power in the Blood.'"

Dagmar also remembers the smells, particularly the soup. Around the Mission, soup was standard fair, and the moniker "soup kitchen" was well deserved. Every day a young Dagmar Edwardson would smell the stock simmering. She reflected with a smile, "Believe me, I can still smell it. To this day I refuse to eat anything resembling soup." But even more overpowering was the smell of coal oil. Dagmar explained, "We had an awful battle with bedbugs in the men's dormitory, and it was a continual day-by-day thing to keep the bedbug population down. They would put the legs of the men's cots in empty sardine tins and fill them with coal oil. The men's dormitory was entirely separate from our living quar-

ters—but it smelled all the time. I found that very difficult, but now when I think of it, it's rather amusing."

Over the years and through all the services, Dagmar
encountered a rich pageantry of humanity. She recalls
with fondness Mr. Selmar the shoemaker, who also
lived at the Mission. He tirelessly worked repairing old
shoes from parts of older shoes. Over the years he
repaired countless pairs of shoes. One annual report
lists 2,319 shoes given out; the majority of these would
have been examined and fixed by Mr. Selmar. He
worked hard. Occasionally he would slip and start
drinking again. Dagmar remembers him, on these rare
occasions, being brought back by the police and
through slurred speech claiming innocence of all
things. He would soon enough mend his ways and
once again begin mending shoes.

Dagmar grew up and lived in the Mission until her
marriage to a young preacher named John
Cunningham. Dagmar reasons that growing up in this
environment had its costs. Reflecting about this she said,
"I sometimes wonder why I never rebelled." One of the
sacrifices was family privacy. To counter this, the
Edwardsons would try to always have breakfast together
as a family. She remembers that it didn't always work
out but the intent and effort were always there. She also
thinks that there were true benefits to her upbringing. "I
didn't know we were poor. It was the way life was. You
learned to accept things the way they were."

She explained that of course not everything
worked out well and not all Mission experiences were
happy ones. Trials were never far off. Dagmar recounts
those early years with genuine joy. "It's not for every-

body, but for me it was a wonderful experience." And when she speaks of her parents there is real admiration. She supposes that her appreciation for her parents has risen over the years as she thinks about the service and sacrifice they took on for the ministry of Hope Mission. She added, "I guess I had a heart for ministry too."

END OF AN ERA

On October 24, 1945, Harold Edwardson called a special meeting of the board. After Mrs. Finlay opened in prayer, Harold informed the board that he and Hillie would be leaving the Mission. After over sixteen years of service, they felt the time for their departure was right for both the Mission and themselves. The board expressed deep regret. The *Edmonton Journal* wrote of their leaving, "They were founders and co-workers in the dispensation of succour to the needy, aid to the sick and aged, relief to many in distress in city and country as well as preachers of the gospel." The article went on to say that the "history of Hope Mission reveals an amazing record of public service."

Another long-term supporter wrote,

I think perhaps we have taken your loyal and efficient, and at times, heart-breaking services for granted and I hope you have not been hurt by this seeming lack of appreciation. To me it has always been a matter of satisfaction that the Trustees of the Tegler Trust were able to avail themselves of your selfless devotion and consecration to the work of the Master.

These were the words of J.F. Lymburn. He had been one of the businessmen who stopped by the little storefront over sixteen years earlier and offered the much needed seed money for the establishment of Hope Mission.

At the meeting Harold told the board that he had discussed the work of the Mission with Rev. Ken Jasper and found that both he and Mrs. Jasper were "keenly interested" in the ministry; because of this he was happy to recommend them as successors in the Mission. This being acceptable, the Edwardsons would stay on for a couple of months to orient the new couple to the ministry of Hope Mission.

When Ken and Helen Jasper were well acquainted with all the facets of the work, Harold and Hillie Edwardson returned to the pastorate. Over the next fifteen years they served churches in Saskatchewan, Alberta and B.C.

Harold Edwardson died in July 1960 in Vancouver. He had been ill during his last few years, but this didn't stop him from conducting large weekly Bible classes. Word of his death reached Edmonton the following Wednesday. The *Edmonton Journal* published the news in an article the following day. Church and social workers called to pay tribute. Mary Finlay was reached for comment. "He was one of the finest and most successful pastoral workers in Western Canada." She went on to describe him as "quite an unusual minister," adding that he was a good Bible teacher and that he had carried on successful pastoral work across the prairies but that he was particularly suited to mission work.

The article mentioned his valuable work through

Hope Mission with the unemployed and hungry, especially during the 1930s. It also brought attention to a further area of compassion he had developed, and that was his special interest and consideration of "the aged and the handicapped." It was noted that in this new and evolving ministry he had provided free lodging and meals for many.

Surviving Harold Edwardson were Mrs. Edwardson, her daughter, Dagmar—by this time married to Rev. John Cunningham and living in Hamilton—and three sons, (Rev.) Paul and the twins, Ray and Ross, who were all living in Vancouver. Hillie remained in Vancouver for the time being but eventually moved back to Edmonton and spent her last years in the Beulah Alliance Senior Citizens Home. She died November 7, 1983. The legacy of Hillie and Harold is one of selfless service, passion for Christ and compassion for the poor, encompassed by stubborn and visionary hope. This legacy is imprinted upon the face of Hope Mission.

Pressing On:
Managing Ministry in
the New World

*Not that I have already obtained this or have
already reached the goal; but I press on to make it
my own, because Christ Jesus has made me his own*
(Philippians 3:12).

REV. KEN AND HELEN JASPER

Rev. Ken Jasper was not a stranger to ministry or to
hard work. While living in Edmonton and working the
night shift as a boilermaker at Gainers, he served as
pastor at a church in Fultonvale, twenty miles east of
the city. Having built the church there, he was open to
a new challenge and a new call. This came with the
invitation from Harold Edwardson to take on the
superintending of Hope Mission. Rev. Jasper had a
heart for working with the poor and had followed with
interest the work of the Mission. His interest in the
Mission and its work, his desire to "win souls" and his
penchant for hard work and a challenge brought him
quite naturally to the leadership of Hope Mission.

These qualities had also endeared him to his church
family, and when he left Fultonvale, many of his

parishioners followed him to Hope Mission to support the work. Lilah Warren (nee Jasper), who lived with her family in the Mission during their ministry, described her dad as "fearless and willing to go anywhere to win a soul."

One Sunday evening after the service, a man appearing to be carrying something suspicious underneath his coat told Rev. Ken Jasper that he would accept Christ if he would meet him at 5:00 a.m. at a particular address on 97 Street. The man had been at the morning service and seemed responsive; he had also confessed some dark event in his past, and now he was strangely anxious to get Ken alone. Two board members who were there that evening took notice and kept the man in their sight as there was reason to believe the man was concealing a weapon. They warned Ken against meeting the man. Ken would have gone alone and precisely at 5:00 a.m.; however, the two board members convinced him to at least wait until a decent hour so they could accompany him.

When they arrived at the prearranged address that morning, no one was there. It was an empty lot. It's only speculation that Ken Jasper was in imminent danger. Whatever the case was that morning, one thing was sure: Rev. Ken Jasper would never have been able to rest had he not gone.

Ken Jasper was from a family of eleven and over the years was able to garner much help from his family. At one time, as many as four other Jaspers, all sisters, were on staff at the Mission. As well, Ken's brother Arthur and his wife, Dorothy, helped to re-establish the Sunday school during this time. This passion for serving and evangelism seemed to run in the Jasper family. Arthur and Dorothy Jasper oversaw the Sunday school for over four years and had the joy of not only caring for kids in need but also "introducing Jesus to many children."

MISSION LIFE

"My parents worked tremendously hard," Lilah Warren (Jasper) said. "On Mondays Mom did the laundry for about thirteen of us, and then she washed and ironed all the sheets and blankets for the men who stayed in the other part of the building. Tuesday was grocery shopping, which was a challenge; then there was cleaning day. Saturday was baking day, and Mom made delicious cinnamon buns and rolls, pies, cakes and all of those delicious goodies. The kitchen with the big black stove smelled so good."

"After the service," Lilah recalled, "the men would gather around long tables for cinnamon buns and coffee. Anyone who came to the door was served." She also remembers that Christmas was made special because her parents made sure that each of the men received a brightly wrapped gift.

Providing the men with serviceable clothing was also part of the ministry. Lilah explained, "Dad drove the 1937 International panel truck picking up the clothing. But one evening when he was coming home, a man who was quite drunk punched out the head-lights in the truck."

Lilah remembered as a little girl in grade 2, "I was terrified of 'drunks' as I childishly called them. When one of them came to the door, I went running up the stairs calling, 'Mom there's a drunk at the door.'"

Growing up in the inner city, Lilah saw the loneliness, desperation and violence first-hand. Every morning as she made her way along the streets to and from her school, which was a couple of blocks away from the Mission, she encountered reminders of the desolation and hardness that the inner city can hold. She said, "Still, seeing all these things around me I somehow knew that God was here too and that he was also with me and with my family."

Lilah Warren recounted, "As my mind goes back to those days of living at the Mission, we really did have some wonderful times. My parents made sure we had our family times too. With four of my aunts and a couple of my uncles helping out at one time or other, we had the support of a big extended family." Through all this Lilah grew to know that God was with the "street" and with the Mission, and she came to see the true value in the care that her parents, along with her aunts and uncles, provided people in need. Lilah concluded that she was enriched by being a part of "a tremendous ministry."

REV. GEORGE AND JOYCE STRICKER

After five years of service, the Jaspers with the consent and approval of the board turned the work of Hope Mission over to Rev. George and Joyce Stricker. Although Rev. Ken and Helen Jasper went on to a new challenge in planning and serving the Richmond Park Tabernacle, they nevertheless stayed connected with the Mission and served on the board for another five years. Clearly they remained interested in the work of the Mission, but they also had an interest in and a desire to support the new supervisory couple since there was a familial connection—Helen Jasper and Joyce Stricker were sisters.

Joyce had lived in the Mission with her sister Helen and brother-in-law Ken a few years before her marriage to George in 1950. She was also there during the time of transition from the Edwardsons to the Jaspers and had opportunity to meet and occasionally be tutored by Mrs. Edwardson.

Some of Joyce's tasks were cleaning, preparing lunches and mending sheets. One day Mrs. Edwardson came by just as Joyce was repairing a tear in an old sheet by sewing some new material over the area. Joyce recalls Mrs. Edwardson's quick but wise advice: "You never sew new material over old." One almost suspects Hillie Edwardson following this up by an explanation of how the material would pull away after the first wash and how this is related to a very instructive story one could find in the Bible (Matthew 9:16-17).

Rev. George Stricker started work at the Mission in the fall of 1951. By the '50s much had changed. World War II was over, and the new world brought a semblance of peace and growing prosperity. The postwar ethos, burgeoning industrialization and its associated economic forces served to quietly curb unemployment and so reduced the need Hope Mission was accustomed to addressing. A board report published in the *Edmonton Journal* on December 11, 1954, shows that the Mission was serving and supplying only 20 percent of what it had provided during the critical needs of the thirties.

For the Mission these were years of adjustment and maintenance in a changing environment. Though the physical needs of previous decades were eased, the spiritual needs were just as great. As always, the Mission held to the simplicity of its regular evening services, because it maintained that the heart of compassion consisted in pointing to the love of Christ while offering what it could in physical nourishment.

SEEDS OF COMPASSION

It was during this time the Strikers became involved with a Métis reserve outside of Edmonton. Early on they had seen a need to try to work more closely with the aboriginal community. It was a difficult task logistically and culturally. They began by simply sending much-needed clothing to the reserve. When they could, they also sent household items, and they opened themselves up to hearing about other needs that the reserve might have. It was a beginning, a seed of an initiative that others from Hope Mission would follow up in the years ahead.

The empathy of the Strikers was also evident when they took in a couple in great need. Joyce recalls that the couple was destitute. To compound the problem, the mother was pregnant with twins. When she delivered the babies, the twins died because of the prolonged malnourished state of the mother. George and Helen cared for the couple through this grievous time and allowed them to stay on at the mission until they were able to get set up in the city. Not only were they helped physically, their experience at the Mission also brought them to put their trust and faith in Jesus Christ. Joyce admitted, "I guess we helped them in a special way."

The ministry of care to people on the street is never without surprises. Even the routine is never routine. Nevertheless, the decade of the fifties saw the Mission move into a somewhat reduced, albeit steady, round of dispensing clothing and other household items; serving meals, lunches and food hampers; giving lodging to men; and occasionally assisting single women. Of course, the Mission continued holding regular evening services and an annual Christmas banquet.

On the surface it was a relatively staid Mission, but the routine wasn't necessarily comfortable. Issues of material and financial support were a concern; and George pressed on and worked hard at procuring what was necessary. And looming was a new and growing problem. The old CNR rooming house on 101 Street, by this time a landmark and home for Hope Mission for thirty years, was rapidly deteriorating.

Standing in the Gap: Years of Challenge

"The rain fell, the floods came, and the winds blew and beat on that house, but it did not fall, because it had been founded on rock" (Matthew 7:25).

DAVID AND ERNA EDEL

David Edel sat in a classroom at Camrose Lutheran College listening to a presentation on the ministry of Hope Mission. As Rev. George Stricker explained both the difficulties and rewards of the work, David found himself unreservedly drawn to the Mission and its way of presenting the gospel through practical service. Several months later, on October 10, 1956, David Edel began his first day as superintendent of Hope Mission. As had become the accepted or perhaps more accurately, *expected*—practice among superintendents' wives, Mrs. Erna Edel also became an employee, with the usual unwritten but all-encompassing job description. The Edels came at a difficult and critical time. Even they didn't know quite what they were up against.

43

TEGLER FOUNDATION

From Hope Mission's inception, the Robert Tegler Trust was a principal financial supporter of the work of the Mission. Because of the interest, devotion and commitment of men like Robert W. Tegler and Alfred Skenfield, Hope Mission had managed to weather some of the more difficult storms during the previous decades. Over the years the trust donated on average 19 to 24 percent of their available funds to Hope Mission. Depending on the year, this worked out to anywhere from $3,000 to $14,000 annually. Considering that the trust helped fund scholarships and contributed to dozens of other charities, Hope Mission obviously held a favoured position with the trustees of the Robert Tegler Trust.

In 1956, the Tegler trustees moved to withdraw their financial support from the Mission. They decided that the deterioration of the Mission's facilities made its maintenance far too costly. It was, in their estimation, a case of throwing away good money. On October 19, 1956, barely a week since becoming supervisor, David Edel found himself, along with a few chosen board members, at a meeting, attempting to persuade the trustees to reconsider their decision. According to the Tegler Trust meeting minutes, as outlined in the *History of the Tegler Foundation,* the delegation headed by a Mr. Arthurs pressed the point that the Mission was still performing a valuable function to needy people, especially at a time when city and provincial welfare bodies had not stepped in to assist. Mr. Arthurs made his appeal as best he could, and the Tegler trustees decided to continue some assistance until the Mission could establish itself with other funding. As a result, the support received from the trust went from several thousand dollars per year to a just few hundred.

Although regular support stopped at the beginning of 1960, the relationship that the Teglers have with Hope Mission remains. In recent years they have generously contributed to various programs and projects that the Mission has initiated. Hope Mission continues to be thankful for the charitable spirit of the people entrusted to manage what was the first established trust in the province of Alberta, now known as the Tegler Foundation.

DESERT

With this new economic reality and the closure of the Mission facility in sight, new strategies and even a renewed vision were needed. Every ministry goes through financial hardship. It's what you might call a *desert* period. It's a time when prayer is focused, faith is stretched and roots sink deeper, a time when inner growth occurs. Despite the very real hurdles in front of them, David Edel and the board were determined to meet the challenges.

Because of the loss of consistent support, the immediate and obvious challenge was financial. As best they could, the board set out to make their need known. Some regular monthly financial support came through a municipal fund known as the Community Chest. As well, during these few years about a dozen local churches contributed when they could. There were always a few hard-earned dollars that came in from personal donations. Occasional gifts-in-kind and breaks from businesses helped out too, but times were lean and "making do" was the modus operandi.

In an effort to build security and commitment, and perhaps in an attempt to enhance its borrowing potential, the board of directors registered Hope Mission with the Societies Branch of Alberta in April 1957. At the same time Hope Mission published a membership offer. Anyone over the age of twenty-one who was interested in the work of Hope Mission could become a voting member of Hope Mission by paying a $5 membership fee—providing that the applicant passed the screening of the board. The board believed that people who became members brought to the Mission a personal commitment towards the work and the life of the ministry. It was the hope that this commitment would bring financial investment.

These were piecemeal initiatives and efforts, but they were just enough—by the grace of God and the prayers and attention of David Edel and the board of directors—to keep the ministry afloat. Clothing was given out, shelter was offered to homeless men, lunches were given to the hungry, needy families were visited, and, with the help of church groups, the gospel was preached at evening services. While those served and cared for were largely unaware of the tenuous state of Hope Mission, God continued to reach into their lives.

HOMELESS

"Hope Mission is without a home" was the opening line of an *Edmonton Journal* news story in early May 1959. The lead continued: "It was turned out of its old building at 10519-101 St., just north of the CNR tracks, April 30, after the structure had been condemned." So it happened that the ministry of the original Mission came to a close, and for the first time in its history, Hope Mission was itself homeless.

Although the rather ignoble end of the Mission was foreseen and understood, for many it was unwelcome news. Losing shelter space was obviously a first-order calamity, but as well, after thirty years in one location, an association with place had inevitably formed. The old converted CNR rooming house had become part of Hope Mission's identity, and it was difficult to see the ministry in a different venue.

The board and David Edel might have been eaten up by anxiety, but they had done some planning and were not caught unawares. Although the Mission's financial state had made it impossible to start a building fund, the director and the board, recognizing the inevitable, had begun to search the downtown for a suitable facility. They found it in a church building on the southwest corner of 104 Avenue and 97 Street. The church was owned by the Plymouth Brethren. "Mission Seeking New Home," an *Edmonton Journal* city section news article, reported, "Hope Mission feels the site is ideal for its work. The property is valued at $50,000, but by special arrangement with its owners, it is available to the Mission for $25,000."

The special arrangement agreed upon was simply that Hope Mission not resell or use the church for anything other than a mission. Having agreed upon this arrangement, Hope Mission began a fundraising drive. Through a special plea campaign to Hope Mission's supporters and friends, a down payment was scraped together. The Mission had also gone cap in hand to City Hall to ask for help in raising the down payment. An incomplete board report related how someone at City Hall—possibly Mr. Elmer Roper, who was the mayor at the time—was sympathetic "but pointed out that the city could not help one religious organization without helping [them] all. He then put his hand in his pocket and gave us $10." This gesture apparently started a small tide of cash and pledges for the Mission. The report concluded, "Several others contributed to the good cause and shortly we had $5,000 to make a down payment on the building." It would seem from other sources that it wasn't quite this easy. Nevertheless, that there was a desire at the municipal level for Hope Mission's viability was something to be thankful and optimistic about.

"Officially Open New Hope Mission for City's Poor"

The down payment was made, a loan was granted through the Treasury Branch, and the property was purchased. On Sunday afternoon, December 20, 1959, Elmer Roper, mayor of Edmonton, flanked by Mary Finlay, David Edel and the minister of pubic welfare, stood in front of a friendly crowd to give greetings and officially open the *new* Hope Mission on 97 Street. Although there was much work to be done in raising an additional $20,000 for the property, it was a good day, a day when Hope Mission could celebrate God's care and provision as it had done many times before. The ministry had a home and could once again serve Edmonton's underprivileged.

The headline in the *Edmonton Sun* that late December day reported "Officially Open New Hope Mission For City's Poor." The sympathetic and prophetic journalist closed his article by saying,

> On Christmas day, when you sit down to that delicious dinner, you will enjoy it more, together with the fellowship of your family, if you recall that you have done what you could afford for the poor and unfortunate people and in obedience to the Lord's words: "Inasmuch as ye have done it unto one of the least of these my brethren, ye have done it unto me." Matt. 25:40.

THE SIXTIES

The sixties were turbulent years for Western society, and no less for Hope Mission. They were years of flux, and the Mission needed people of courage and stability to stand in the gaps and brave the maelstroms. Having taken a step of faith and passed the initial obstacles of change, Hope Mission was now confronted with the question of "life after."

No doubt the transition was something of a watershed time for board members. Several members considered this a time to allow others to invest new energy and ideas into Hope Mission. They had served faithfully for many years and saw the events surrounding the facility changeover as a kind of fitting conclusion to their service. This eventually resulted in a near wholesale turnover of the board of directors. Four out of six board members resigned. Among them was Mary Findlay, whose resignation letter, dated September 3,

1959, was written thirty years almost to the day of Hope Mission's inception.

As new board members came on to replace vacancies left by resignations, they were immediately challenged by the question "How do you keep a ministry viable through major transition and change at the threshold of a new, uncertain decade?" In the first few months of 1960, it was apparent as revealed through board meeting minutes that although hopes were still high, there was clear concern about the Mission's stability.

The impossibility of maintaining the Mission's leased neon sign almost seemed a harbinger of demise. It was a splendid sign that brightly read "Hope Mission—Christ Died for Our Sins." The neon sign was leased sometime in the mid-fifties, but even with the goodwill and patience of Blanchett Neon Ltd., Hope Mission was unable to renew the $12.50 per month contract. The simple loss of the lighted neon sign said volumes about what board members were reluctant to say out loud— that the future of the Mission was in doubt.

But uncertainty is not always bad. It imposes a dependence on God's provision that is not always felt during a time of balanced budgets and secured funding. With this understanding the board ended their first meeting of the decade with a commitment to "a more definite period of prayer to be set aside regularly by the board."

"Hope Mission Helps 50 Needy Nightly"

During the few brief months that Hope Mission was without a facility, the Mission still found ways to help the poor through co-operation with other agencies. At the very least they were able to distribute clothing to those in need. Now in their new premises, they could get down to the work of evening gospel services with a lunch, clothing distribution, and meeting other requests for help. On February 3, 1960, the *Edmonton Journal* ran the article "Hope Mission Helps 50 Needy Nightly." Commenting on the valuable work the Mission was once again carrying out seven days a week, the charitable journalist outlined why the Mission needed donors and where donations should be sent. The article was more a veiled or indirect plea for funds and was probably solicited by the Mission. In any case, the word needed to go out that Hope Mission was itself in great need.

A few months following the opening of the new facility, the Mission found itself failing to carry its debt. They were unable to pay the caretaker's stipend, let alone the Edels' small salary. And they were in danger of missing mortgage payments. In a desperate move letters were sent out to local churches disclosing what other churches, twelve in total, had given to the work of the Mission over the past three years. The range of individual church giving was from $10 to $275. The letter was a no-holds-barred entreaty. It ended in two sentences, both in uppercase: "WE NEED YOUR HELP TODAY. TOMORROW MAY BE TOO LATE."

The treasurer, Ron Gillespie, who would resign a month later because of health problems, sent out special appeal letters to all regular supporters, relating the sense of urgency. In the general report of April 1960, having itemized the help given out for the month and noting that "3 decisions for Christ were made," Chairman K. R.

Wallgren included this statement: "We covet your prayers that we may stand together and see God's deliverance at this time of our financial CRISIS."

From the perspective of Hope Mission it was a financial crisis; and from the perspective of the Edels it was, in some sense, too late. A most difficult decision needed to be made. At a board meeting on May 20, 1960, it was moved, seconded and carried that "due to financial circumstances, Brother and Sister Edel be relieved of their obligation as superintendents of the Mission." Other than extending David and Erna a "hearty expression of thanks," it was all the Mission could do to send them off with a few household effects—a vacuum cleaner and floor polisher.

The Edels had been on a salary of subsistence for most of their tenure. The fact that for the first time the Mission was unable to pay a superintendent a nominal wage was clearly a low point in the history of Hope Mission. It was under these conditions that Rev. A. L. Sanderson was to assume the supervisory duties of the Mission. This role was on top of his administrative obligations of a board member and, since the departure of Mr. Ron Gellespie, the obligations of treasurer. But the Mission would remain indebted to the Edels for their loyalty, faithfulness, enduring service and, as the minutes understatedly concluded, "especially under great difficulties and trying times."

Rev. Alex L. Sanderson

Through the sixties there were many occasions of shared responsibility in the supervisory role of Hope Mission. Board members pitched in and served as they were needed. Sustained and overall leadership came through Rev. Alex Sanderson. With the approval of the board he was asked to assume the position of acting superintendent until such a time that the Mission could once again afford to hire a supervisor.

Rev. Sanderson, born in 1900, was a retired United Church minister and had been a board member since the mid-fifties. He was also the president of the temperance association, and as such he had been challenged early on to establish a more direct ministry to alcoholics. It was his vision that the new facility be used in some way as an outreach to those caught in this addiction. With this motivation he had devoted considerable energy in making arrangements for the acquisition of the building on 97 Street.

Rev. Sanderson's vision looked toward the establishment of what he wanted to call The Hope Centre for Alcoholics. He initiated a campaign called the Seven Year Plan. It was a kind of marketing strategy that entailed a mail-out of what were made to look like award certificates. On the certificate was the bold caption "Builder of Hope Mission." It was left to the donor to decide how much of a builder he or she wanted to be by checking the box beside the chosen amount. There was hope for the campaign, but for some reason it didn't generate the desired enthusiasm or cash.

Coinciding with this effort, board members approached Mr. Jorgenson, then Minister of Welfare, and courted his department for support. A few months later Rev. Sanderson received the disappointing news that his proposal would not be accepted. There was a suggestion that the province might help with some

provisional operating funding, but the board understood this intimation to be more of a courtesy than
anything else.

By the summer of 1967 the directors recognized
that the Mission would have to move again. The
church building was old, and despite care and paint it
was coming to the end of its life. More significantly,
there were strong indications coming from city hall
that the property was slated for expropriation. In light
of this Rev. Sanderson put together a committee to prepare for the venture. The committee was led by Dr.
Wahl, a professor at North American Baptist College.
His active and practical involvement as a Hope Mission
board member and volunteer was his way of giving balance to the world of academia that surrounded him. Dr.
Wahl researched and compiled a comprehensive report
on the state of Hope Mission, detailing what would be
needed and desired in a new facility and the accompanying programs. The report also included how the
Mission was to be staffed and financed.

A clear attempt was made to keep the report on
"The Future and Expansion of Hope Mission" within
reach. In addition to the Mission's present activities the
report foresaw a women's ministry division, a coordinated ministry to boys and girls, a shelter for men and
women, an expanded counselling service that included
assistance in job skills and finding employment, a
halfway house for a new prison ministry, and of course
a facility to accommodate it all. The report, as noted in
the minutes, "seemed beyond our reach, but on the
other hand if we once have the mind of God in what
He desires to do, nothing is impossible to Him." For the

time being the report had more visionary value than anything else, but it did represent the old faith that Hope Mission was founded on.

This was the second time Rev. Sanderson had prepared for a transition. Although his Hope Centre for Alcoholics didn't materialize, his quiet intensity and careful leadership kept the Mission from floundering and perhaps folding. Because of this, his dream of a direct and specific ministry for alcoholics was realized in the coming years and actualized beyond his own expectations.

To the expressed regret of all board members, Rev. Sanderson resigned from Hope Mission on December 30, 1969, and moved back to Ontario. Herb Jamieson, the chairman at the time, remembers Rev. Alex Sanderson: "I knew him well, and I had great respect for him. He kept the Mission open; if it wasn't for him during this time we would have had to close it down." Mrs. McMinn, secretary and voluntary bookkeeper for the Mission during Rev. Sanderson's time of service, had this to say: "Alex didn't like doing books, so when he became Hope Mission treasurer, I helped him out. He wasn't really a boss; he was more of a friend. You could tell he cared for people, especially poorer people. And he lived his Christian principals."

MISSION MANNA

Although Hope Mission's viability during these years was precarious, at crucial times it was often on the receiving end of providential blessings. After the Second World War, the Canadian government found itself with large caches of food surpluses. In the succeeding years of the cold war the federal government held on to these surpluses as a contingency. By the mid-sixties it was decided that it was time to dispose of the stockpiles. Hope Mission, one of the many social agencies contacted, accepted a truckload of canned meat. It was Spork, Canada's answer to America's Spam.

The Spork was something of a mother lode, yet the difficulty faced was finding appropriate storage space. Because the church that now housed the Mission was originally built for a Baptist congregation, it naturally had a large baptistery—a large tank where a candidate is led down steps to stand in chest-high water to then be fully immersed by the pastor. The baptistery made a fine storehouse and was filled to overflowing with the ageless meat. No doubt the thousands of tins were properly blessed.

Herb Jamieson said that for several years the Mission served Spork sandwiches after the nightly service. By then some of the men and women who were regulars at the services probably considered the Spork sandwich a veiled blessing. The canned meat finally ran out, but the board, undeterred by a few Spork murmurings, contacted federal government surplus to see if they still had any left. Unfortunately for the Mission, but perhaps fortunately for its patrons, the government had given away their last tin quite some time before their call.

Attitude Check

At one point the Mission employed an individual named John. John was an all-purpose staff person, a custodian, street liaison, counsellor, manager, security guard and the only other staff member outside of the acting supervisor. During the early years in the 97 Street mission, the board was unable to pay any kind of a wage. In exchange for his services, John was allowed to live in the Mission's kitchen, which was the only appropriate living space. It was a mutually beneficial and agreed upon arrangement that helped keep the Mission doors open.

Over the months, the inner city disturbances of early morning raps on the Mission door, broken bottles and occasional sirens wore on John's nerves and patience. Because of these irritants and his dissatisfaction with having only his room and board taken care of, he finally offered his resignation. The board certainly would have been delighted to pay him, but that was a current impossibility and had in any case not been the agreed-upon arrangement.

Having no one in the wings, the board declined his resignation and asked him to stay on. He could, of course, have simply walked out. Instead, sensing his position of being able to apply a certain degree of pressure, he offered his resignation again the following month with the thought that it might be met with an offer of money. Yet the situation hadn't changed, and again the resignation was refused and he was asked to stay on. The offering of his resignation and it being turned down became monthly practice, until one month his resignation was accepted.

For John the unexpected breaking of this custom came as something of a shock. His concerns were no doubt valid, but as it was explained, such hardships are part of ministry, and ministry is never advanced when we put ourselves before the work or when service is done grudgingly or manipulatively. As was conveyed to John, true and loving service is always shown in attitude. The Mission carried on without John.

PORTRAITS OF GRACE

The real work of the Mission was that every labour and every act of service be carried out in the name of Christ. The *real* work is the entire spectrum of tasks, from the washing of a floor to the drafting of a director's strategic plan, from a chaplain's counselling session to an administrative memo, from the preparation of a sandwich to the prayer with a parolee. The goal of all this work is in Jesus' answer to John the Baptist. John asked Christ if he was the one, or should he wait for another. Christ said, *"The blind receive their sight, the lame walk, the lepers are cleansed, the deaf hear, the dead are raised, and the poor have good news brought to them"* (Matthew 11:5). This is the raison d'être of every act of love. Everything undertaken in the love of Christ collaborates with the Spirit of Jesus in drawing people to his side, in giving them new life and sustaining them as portraits of grace.

In March 1967, a native man named Walter stopped in at a meeting, where he heard the good news of Jesus Christ. He opened his heart, and his life changed. Board member Bryn Skagen talked to him that evening. Walter confessed that he planned to end his own life that night, but when he had been walking past the Mission, he found himself drawn inside. There, he heard news and found a person who literally saved his life. Walter became a fixture around the Mission for some time. He would often be seen at the evening services talking to others, explaining with joy what had happened to him.

Through the late sixties a thriving Sunday school program was maintained by Miss Windum and several volunteers. Most of the children were of Métis and Chinese origin. Every Sunday afternoon—later expanded to include Saturday mornings—forty or more children from the inner city would gather to hear Bible stories, complete a lesson and then have some refreshments. One Sunday Miss Windum was interrupted by one of the older girls just before she began with the Sunday school lesson. The girl inquired if it might be possible for the lesson that day to be postponed. When Miss Windum asked the reason for this request, the girl replied, "Because me and my two friends want to pray and accept Jesus in our hearts."

<h3 style="text-align:center">HAROLD BURMA</h3>

Harold Burma's arrival on the board in 1959 had the effect of adding a bit more exposure for Hope Mission. Harold loved to sing and play guitar, and along with his wife Victoria and his sister Anne he formed what was known as the Gospel Tone Trio. Every Sunday afternoon at 2:30, CFCW in Camrose brought to its listening audience the *Mission Hour Broadcast.* The broadcast drew a following and managed to maintain itself during these years. Many in the Edmonton area tuned in to hear the gospel in musical form. The broadcast was carried from 1959 to July 1966, when a lack of support forced the program off the air. Over the years the Gospel Tone Trio also produced four long-play vinyl records. For Hope

Mission, the broadcast attracted some supporters who contributed to the work of the Mission long after the program was off the air.

Harold Burma went on to serve two terms as board chairman, his last term ending in 1992. Harold continues to serve the Mission in the way he originally came to it. Once a month you can still find him singing, playing and sharing the gospel with the men and women who come to the Mission's evening service. It's something he still loves to do. He finds motivation in those who occasionally respond to the message of Jesus.

One such occasion that stands out and has stayed with Harold over many years was the evening that Jim Auger came to know Christ. Harold was in the habit of singing six songs with his worship team and then speaking briefly on the message the songs conveyed. They would then sing another set of songs. On this particular night in 1972, just as Harold was about to start to sing again, a young native man walked to the front, fell on his knees and, with his face pressed into the floor of the platform, wept profusely and cried out to receive Jesus Christ. Harold hadn't made an altar call. Harold recalled that the man "was simply called by Christ...and his face was washed with tears." After praying, Harold struggled to finish the service. "I was choked up and on the edge of tears myself. After the service, the joy he had was something beyond words." Harold added, "For months I too felt the joy of Christ because of what happened to this man."

For a short time Jim stayed around and helped out at the Mission. Harold noticed that "he would simply beam as he swept the floor of the old Mission basement." But Jim had a very troubled and broken background, and Harold wondered what would happen to him. Four months after moving away from the Mission, Jim called Harold at his work to tell him he had the $3 he had borrowed from him for bus fare to go see his family, and he wanted to meet him to pay him back. He then exclaimed, to Harold's great delight, "And I'm still serving the Lord."

Two decades later Harold again met Jim, this time at a Hope Mission banquet put on for the inner-city community. It seemed to Harold that Jim had seen some struggles, but Jim made a point of telling Harold that he was still living the Christian life.

Jim's story in some sense typifies the intent and the hope of the ministry of Hope Mission. Jim had changed, and even though he had most everything going against him and very little support and no doubt had his continual struggles, he did his best to follow Christ and live out the message of the gospel.

HERB JAMIESON

Of the many people associated with Hope Mission over the years perhaps Herb Jamieson is the one most recognized. Herb was born and raised in Saskatoon, Saskatchewan. A childhood bout of polio, which disabled his left arm, did nothing to compromise his inner drive. After completing high school, he moved to Vegreville and got a job managing the hardware division of Macleods. He worked there through 1931 and 1932 and then moved to Edmonton to become an employee of Northern Hardware.

In Edmonton he began to attend Beulah Alliance under the pastoral guidance of Rev. Gordon Schitch. In 1935, after anguished self-reflection "under the tender conviction of Christ," as Herb put it, "and seeing myself as a defeated young man," he gave himself to the Lord and "never looked back." Henrietta, whom Herb had first met in high school in Saskatoon, was attending Beulah at the same time. He married Henrietta in 1936.

Herb's first exposure to Hope Mission came only days after he became a Christian. With a few friends from Beulah, he went down to the Mission one evening simply to observe. He remembers descending the stairs into a dimly lit basement where the service was held. Because of his own early ties with Saskatoon, Herb recalls easily that it was a retired schoolteacher from Saskatoon that addressed the crowd that evening. The service and the setting left an impression. In the faces of some of these men, Herb recognized his former self.

Herb would soon leave Edmonton. His reputation as a good "hardware man" preceded him, and for his new employer the fact that he was a Christian also weighed in his favour. As a result he accepted a job in Meeting Creek managing the hardware division of Progress Lumber. In Meeting Creek's Mission Covenant Church, under the pastoral care of Rev. Clarence Strom—brother to future premier Harry Strom—the Jamiesons found even greater Christian fellowship and their Christian formation took on a clearer significance. As Herb described it, "The church was on fire, and it was as though the town was on fire, and we were there, on fire too."

Herb soon entertained the thought of going to Bible school and the possibility of becoming a pastor. His desire was God, and he craved to know all of God's Word and find God's total will for his life. From Meeting Creek to a country store near Wetaskiwin, Herb's industry finally allowed him to go to Bible school in Prince Albert. Although he left school before graduating, he was called to pastor a Mission Covenant church in Kenistino, Saskatchewan. Herb served as pastor there for two years.

Herb Jamieson moved back to Alberta with his growing family and took a job managing a co-op store in Lamont. Again, Herb's skill and workmanship did not go unnoticed. He was offered a partnership in an insulation business. He accepted and a year later bought the business. Within a year he sold it and moved back to Edmonton. Because of his knowledge of the hardware trade and his ability with people, Herb was always able to find work. He worked briefly for Eaton's and then Woodwards but eventually "took the plunge" and bought a store on Stony Plain Road. It became Jamieson Hardware. "It had the biggest sign on Stony Plain Rd with a picture of a man hammering a nail. It was a grand sign."

In June 1959, Herb ran for public office. He succeeded in becoming a member for the legislative assembly (MLA) for Alberta in the constituency of Jasper West. He served one term, June 18, 1959, to June 27, 1963, under Premiere Ernest Manning. He declined to run again. It wasn't just the politics; to Herb during this time, "things began to go sour." The hardware store, through a zoning fiasco, was not doing well either. Yet Herb soldiered on. A few years later he was asked to run for a school trustee position. He lost the first election, then won the second and served as trustee for twelve years.

With Herb moving back to Edmonton it was not long before he reconnected with Hope Mission. He began to take an evening service once a month. Mrs. Velma Mark, another valuable long-term volunteer, helped him out by playing piano and organ. Herb served the Mission in this way for over ten years. During this time he also became a board member. He doesn't remember a specific time or indeed any formal installation as a board member. As he put it, "It used to be that if you showed up at a meeting you were on the board." Herb showed up at his first Hope Mission board meeting sometime in 1960.

He served faithfully during the next several years and on February 25, 1969, led his first meeting as Hope Mission's chairman. The theme of his devotional that day was appropriately taken from Ezra 7:10. *"For Ezra had prepared his heart to seek the law of the LORD, and to do it"* (KJV). Preparation of heart was needed as the board looked toward the coming decade, because it would take a secure faith to persevere during those thin years.

Hope Mission was still touching lives by feeding the hungry and caring for souls, but from an organizational and financial standpoint the Mission's future still looked precarious. Herb called it "shaky" and added, "It was more than shaky; it was like nothing on earth." During this time there were certain efforts and forces at work to bring the Mission under a particular denomination. Hope Mission has always been, as it was set out to be, interdenominational. Nevertheless, it was understandable that with the looming financial clouds some saw the umbrella of a single committed denomination as security. This was not to be; the original vision of a cross-section of primarily evangelical churches coming together to govern and support the Mission was upheld. The push to a single denominational tie never graduated to the form of a motion. To ensure this would never happen, at the annual general meeting in 1971, under Herb's chairmanship, a new bylaw was struck that there could be no more than three board members from one denomination or assembly. In conjunction with this, the bylaw limiting the maximum number of board members to fourteen was amended to seventeen.

It was Herb's heart and vision for ministry that brought him repeatedly back to the Mission. His scope of involvement was from the "front lines" to board chairman. The personal manner of his service was infectious. For any who knew him, he was a champion of Hope Mission, an advocate for the people the Mission served, and a catalyst that brought many to happy involvement with the Mission. Bruce Reith, the current director, said, "Herb was a true mentor."

Herb Jamieson passed away in September 2003. He was ninety-one years old. He will be remembered as a man of integrity, great faith, clear conviction, open compassion, sweet disposition and genuine joy. As a friend of the poor and neglected, he was known to many as Mr. Hope Mission.

BRYN SKAGEN

Bryn Skagen never cared to be out front. His passion was the gospel and working wherever there was a need, and it was Hope Mission's privilege to be the vehicle to help carry out his passion. Mr. Skagen was invited to join the board in 1960. He was seventy-six years old when he joined Hope Mission, and he served until 1972, when he turned eighty-eight. While active in other ministries and in his church, on top of his duties as board member he gave his energy in voluntarily overseeing Hope Mission's Sunday school program. In the summer of 1968, Bryn made it possible for sixteen children from his Sunday school program to go to a summer camp at Ross Haven. This was the first time that Hope Mission became involved in summer camp ministry. Reflected in the minutes that fall was the observation that all sixteen children had behaved very well. For Bryn, this observation was greatly eclipsed by the revelation that all sixteen had accepted Christ.

Over the years it was evident that teaching Sunday school and serving children was what Bryn loved, but he agonized over what he felt was a lack of results. Because he himself chose to live in the inner city with the people he served, he saw first-hand that what he tried to instill in young lives was quickly undermined by unstable home conditions.

Bryn Skagen had been a sailor with the Royal Canadian Navy. He served in the two great military conflicts of the 20th century. Perhaps it was because of his career with the navy that Bryn never married. However, he took his role as board member very seriously. He was something of a prophet. Issues of motivation, loyalty and values were very important to him. He also loved to read and study the Bible, and he had developed a firm grasp of Reformation theology. For

Bryn, to know where one stood was a primary concern. His views were no doubt uncomfortably rigid at times, but issues of principle were never overlooked. For example, it was at Bryn's insistence that the words *in repentance* were added to one of the clauses in Hope Mission's statement of faith. It would now read, "And all who in repentance receive him by faith as Saviour and Lord are justified through His shed blood."

After studying some of the newer Bible translations that began to appear, Bryn Skagen became quite disturbed. For him, the King James Version was clearly a superior translation, and he unequivocally made his view known to the board. In a letter he encouraged the board to examine and "carefully compare [the other translations] with the Authorized Version and note the wide divergence." He was fixed in his opinion and even convinced the board to include a statement that "The Society favours the use of the King James Version of the scriptures," in Hope Mission's statement of faith. In a follow-up letter he expressed that he still felt this was "too vague." Left to him, he would have made it mandatory that all preaching and teaching in the Mission be done exclusively with the King James Bible in hand. The King James qualification has since disappeared from the statement of faith. Today we might see Bryn as a curiosity and dismiss his view as narrow; at the time, rightly or wrongly, it was his undivided love of God's Word that compelled him to take a stand.

In private Bryn was quiet, but he held his own as a public speaker. This talent, as well as his theological knowledge, allowed him to guest preach and teach at various churches, and he was a frequent speaker on a

radio program called *The Reformation Hour.* Bryn
Skagen's love of Scripture and theology also came out
in poetry. When the board chairman, Herb Jamieson,
asked Bryn to prepare a devotional on a particular
theme for a board meeting, Bryn came back with a
detailed study of the Jewish religious understanding
and the Christian implications of the Old Testament
tabernacle, plus a theologically packed poem worthy of
a hymnbook:

THE TABERNACLE IN THE WILDERNESS

The Tabernacle of the Lord, upon the desert
sand,
Is still the only way there is into Immanuel's
land.
For there upon the Holy mount, and by His own
dear hand,
The pattern once for all He drew, for evermore
to stand.

The Brazen Altar first of all, a sinner, I must see,
For 'tis the Cross of Calvary, where Jesus died for
me;
And there the blood, His precious blood, was
shed upon the tree,
That now my soul, by faith in Him, from doom
and Hell set free.

The cleansing Laver farther on, a daily stopping
place;
Is needed for my walk with Him, and for my
growth in grace.

Each day to meet Him in His work, and there
before His gaze,
Unfold my heart for Him to see, while I behold
His face.

Man shall not live by bread alone, but shall by
every word
That God hath spoken, feast and know the Table
of the Lord.
In unison with Him commune, in loving one-
ness there,
With other gladsome hearts enjoy, the
Shewbread of His care.

The Golden Candlestick, the Light, and this is
also He,
Who by His Spirit thus will give, to me, yes even
me
Such Light that shall His own reflect, contin-
uing to be,
That these without, in Him alone the greater
Light shall see.

The Golden Altar ever stands with incense sweet
ascending,
My Saviour, and my High Priest there, on my
behalf attending.
His interceding cannot fail, because He ever
liveth,
And when by faith I praise and pray, the victory
He giveth.

Before the throne of God' own grace, the blessed
Mercy Seat,
Clad in my Saviour's righteousness, He there
with me do meet;
Presenting there His promises, as He shall will
and guide,
I bless His name forevermore, and there in Him
abide.

(This poem was written in June 1970. Over the
years, Bryn wrote many such poems and late in
his life took the time to compile them into
book form.)

In June 1974, the board of Hope Mission and others
gathered to celebrate Mr. Skagen's ninetieth birthday.
He was given a life membership certificate. Maynard
Cole, a volunteer who worked under his direction, said
of Bryn, "He was a simple man and a kind man; he was
also very generous. Once he bought all of us volunteers
beautiful hard cover Scofield Bibles. He did things like
that." Bryn Skagen's long and energetic life was
devoted to the Lord. At a time when most people
would long since have been retired, Bryn entered
another arena of Christian service in Hope Mission.

MARTHA PEHL

Martha Pehl was the quintessential Mission volunteer. She was a tireless worker with little patience for
laziness. Martha was strong minded, strong willed and
seemingly impervious to the sights, smells and sounds
of inner-city ministry. She also exemplified an unam-
biguous devotion to her God.

Martha served through a succession of supervisors, from the late sixties to the late eighties. Through much of this time, she daily volunteered her time and energy. She made sandwiches, sorted donations of all kinds, and was always cleaning. Director Ray Buttery recalled one story that exemplifies Martha's heart and will. It involved a fairly brash prostitute who was well known to the Mission.

The woman came to the back door of the Mission one day in urgent need of the washroom. She made it to the bottom of the stairs and, unable to contain herself any longer, urinated all over the floor. After helping the woman clean herself, Martha got a mop and a pail of hot water. With deliberate efficiency, she cleaned up the mess, and since the pail did not have a wringer attachment, she wrung it out with her hands. It was the kind of act she practised routinely.

Martha was unusually industrious and frugal. She raised her children and paid for a house while working variously as maid and dishwasher. At a critical time in 1974, as industrious as she was, she was able to loan the Hope Mission $10,000. It was her idea; it was her loan, and she gave it interest free but with one small condition. If she died before the Mission could pay it back, the loan would be forgiven in full, but the Mission would cover all funeral expenses.

Straining Forward: Re-evaluations and Revisions

But this one thing I do: forgetting what lies behind and straining forward to what lies ahead (Philippians 3:13).

THE OLD CHURCH ON THE CORNER

Elmer Roper was the mayor of Edmonton from 1960 to 1963. During his tenure he instituted a "renewal program," the intent of which was to update and beautify the city's downtown. As a result, under the subsequent administration of Mayor Iver Dent, the city began proceedings to expropriate Hope Mission's aging and by the city's renewal standards *unlovely* church hall. However the directors of Hope Mission were already aware of the city's plan. Former mayor Elmer Roper had alerted the board that the old church on 97 Street was on the list for expropriation. In time the property, along with other property west of the church, would be used to accommodate a new and expanded post office. Once again, the leadership of Hope Mission was called to make a decision that required foresight braced by a belief that God wanted the Mission to carry on.

In some sense the Mission didn't have an option. While there might have been a few more years of service left in the "old church on the corner," it was already apparent that Hope Mission needed more space to accommodate the numbers of (mostly) men who needed help. The board could wait it out and cast themselves on the city's benevolence until they found a spot selling for approximately the sum they would receive from the sale of the facility. Or they could begin to take steps, relying on God to steer them as they went. They decided to take the small step of starting a building fund, and two years later, in the spring of 1969, they began looking in earnest for a new site.

Merging Missions

In April 1969, Hope Mission's building committee viewed a property at 96 Street and 101 Avenue. Its location and size were appropriate; however, there was need of considerable renovation. The board minutes pointed out that "we must have assurance that this is the Lord's time and place, thus we must continue to wait upon Him." On the heels of this prospect, in June 1969, Hope Mission was approached by an agency called Turning Point and asked to consider a kind of partnership.

Turning Point was a treatment program and ministry to alcoholics. Because there were plans to develop Turning Point into a full residential program, it had purchased a large three-storey building. But it also had an accompanying financial burden. As well, they had just come through an internal reorganization made necessary by fraud and embezzlement. The result left

Turning Point in financial straits and, according to one Hope Mission board member, "with a backlog of questionable reputation." Another concern was that the restructuring of Turning Point also resulted in turning away from a faith-based approach of helping alcoholics to primarily a medical and scientific approach, an approach that at the time was gaining a great deal of academic support.

Hope Mission was not opposed to new researched avenues of addressing addictions. The board's concern and caution was with the apparent separation of physical and mental wellness from spiritual healing. This divorcing of body from soul ultimately undermines the core of Hope Mission's profession. As a result, when Hope Mission was sought out as a possible suitor for the troubled agency, the board of directors were understandably wary. The Mission was in need of a building, and by all accounts Turning Point's facility offered great potential; but as the minutes from June 10, 1969 recount, "with the present stigma attached to the name 'Turning Point' and the possibility of unbelievers becoming involved, we needed to exercise much prayerful consideration before making moves towards joining with them." Subsequently, no immediate move was made. Regardless of the desirability of even the best facility, merging with an agency that had the residue of scandal   and in the board's view a questionable philosophy   was too great a price to pay.

Hope Mission had a strong interest in working to rehabilitate addicts and alcoholics, and they particularly wanted to be able to follow up with the men who made a profession of faith and needed this kind of help. This was, after all, a long-time dream of Rev. Sanderson's, but the Mission had never been able to acquire a building specifically for this kind of ministry. In a second overture to Hope Mission, Turning Point invited the board to view a vacant building known as the Windsor Rooms that was owned by the city. Some renovations were needed for it to pass fire code, but these were assessed as being manageable. When the collective delegation went to view the facility, they were unable to gain entrance because they couldn't find the right key.

On October 28, 1969, a special meeting of both boards was called to discuss the possibility of developing a joint Christian rooming centre. Rev. Alex Sanderson was one of the team from Hope Mission who had been delegated to go and inspect the building and assess its suitability. He told the gathering that he had been doing a lot of praying and seeking "that the Lord would guide as to what should be done." When this settled on the ears of all present, he added, "The very fact that it had been impossible for us to find the proper key and get into the building seemed to indicate that the Lord was not opening the door in this direction at the present." The meeting was adjourned, but not before noting that both sides had a mutual concern for this kind of ministry and that this would "spur them on to more fervent prayer" for the meeting of this need.

Less than two weeks later Turning Point was forced to vacate their building, and their work came to an end. However, Hope Mission's brief association with Turning Point did have a positive consequence. In a month Rev. Sanderson would leave and the Mission would be in urgent need of a capable supervisor and director. Howard Hunt, a staff member at Turning Point, had been in conversation with Hope Mission throughout the merger exploration. Howard, in reference to the Windsor Rooms, had described his own deep commitment to founding a Christian residential center for men caught in addiction. Through this and other exchanges the board saw in him a Christlike desire to serve and a genuine heart for Mission ministry. When Turning Point closed, the board decided to contact Mr. Hunt to ask him to consider taking on the responsibility of supervisor of Hope Mission.

A New Home

Things now happened quickly. In late November 1969, a property at 106 Avenue and 99 Street came up for sale. The property was comprised of four lots occupied by a large house formerly used as a parsonage, a smaller cottage and a large wood-frame church. Originally built as a Presbyterian church, it had been sold to the Christian Reform congregation, which now wanted to relocate.

The board wasted little time in contacting the owners of the Third Christian Reform Church. The initial meeting went well. They had listed their property for $125,000 and already had fielded inquiries and interest from a few organizations and businesses, but they preferred to sell to someone like Hope Mission because, as one of their delegates said, "They would know that it would continue to be used in the work of the Lord." For this reason they would be prepared to offer the property to Hope Mission for $100,000 dollars. The Mission was unable to make any concrete offer, and the meeting was concluded with a "gentleman's agreement" that they would be in touch soon and that neither side would make further moves without notifying the other.

Because of the location and the size of the property, the board believed that in spite of financial contraindications the property would be key to the expansion of the ministry of Hope Mission. With this vision, the board began to pray for "someone with a burden upon their heart to such an extent that they were willing to give themselves wholeheartedly to its promotion." Herb Jamieson was given the task of making contact with Howard Hunt as a possible candidate to fill this role.

Hope Mission notified city hall that they had found the place where they believed their work could continue and be enhanced and that therefore they were ready to sell the Mission hall. An appraisal was done, and the property's worth was established at between $70,000 and $80,000. Hope Mission had a good relationship with the city and had no trouble in asking for the higher figure for their property. In fact, according to one account it was former Mayor Roper who encouraged the board to ask for the higher price. There were some who evidently had a soft spot in their hearts for Hope Mission. Even the bill Hope Mission received from the appraiser had been reduced to a token amount.

Having sold the old Mission for $80,000, Hope Mission was in the position to purchase the new property at 98 Street and 106 Avenue. The agreed upon price was $100,000 dollars. Hope Mission paid $65,000 cash, and the Reform church agreed that the balance of $35,000 would be paid by the end of 1971. In this way the Christian Reform church was still able to use the sanctuary on occasion. The opening ceremony for the Mission's new home was held on Sunday, September 12, 1970, and a new phase began for Hope Mission.

PRAYER AND PROVISIONS

The years were still lean and held promise only for those with eyes of faith. There was no money for extras and barely enough for necessities. Nevertheless, small miracles, the kind that add up, kept occurring. A month or so after opening, the Mission received a vital and symbolic gift from an anonymous donor. It was a large freezer. Mrs. Relf, the wife of the acting supervisor, was particularly thankful but didn't hesitate to pray "that He who had so wonderfully provided would also fill it in His own way." It was a prayer reminiscent of George Mueller's, with the result that the very next day a delivery truck arrived with foodstuffs that filled the new freezer to overflowing.

These little miracles were needed because by November 1971, Hope Mission had little more than the $10,000 they had reserved at the time of the purchase. They needed another $25,000 to retire the debt as promised to the Third Christian Reform Church. This was a daunting sum of money. Percy Herring, acting as Hope Mission's legal council, encouraged the board to meet with the Third Christian Reform Church as soon as possible.

During this time Herb Jamieson also solicited the appropriate government departments to see if a grant might be forthcoming. He prepared a short proposal, laying out the work of the Mission, and sent it to the Hon. Ray Speaker, who at that time was minister of health and social development. However, in a return letter to Herb Jamieson, Mr. Speaker responded that his department did not consider giving grants to organizations such as Hope Mission. The response wasn't totally unexpected, but given the circumstances at the Mission, it was obviously disheartening.

Consequently, in January 1972, a special executive meeting was called. The directors decided on a campaign to sell debentures at 8 percent in an effort to raise the final amount. In the ensuing two months there were few takers. Being in arrears now for several months was weighing heavily on the board. The Christian Reform Church leaders had been patient, but they were now communicating their concern through their lawyer.

Mission executives went to the Treasury Branch but were refused a loan. Next they approached the Bank of Montreal. They were told that they needed ten co-signers for a loan to be granted. Risking their own livelihoods, the board led by Herb Jamieson came together to meet the bank's demand for co-signatories. A mortgage was granted, the church was paid, and in the end the money received from the sale of debentures was returned with interest to the handful of purchasers.

MR. AND MRS. NORMAN RELF

Superintendents and directors of Hope Mission have always been people of unique character and independent spirit. The volatilities and vagaries encountered in

Mission work necessitate such traits in its leaders. These peculiarities of inner-city ministry suited the character of Norman Relf. Even before he became involved in Hope Mission it was evident that he had a zeal for evangelism. In something that echoed the foolish boldness of St. Francis, Norman would walk the downtown core wearing a sandwich board. One side declared, "I'm a fool for Christ's sake"; the reverse side asked, "Whose fool are you?" As you might expect, this attracted a wide array of reactions. Whatever the response, it was Norman's great privilege to try to turn all openings and exchanges into a presentation of the gospel.

Norman Relf joined the board sometime in the mid-sixties. When Rev. Alex Sanderson resigned at the end of 1969, Norman was asked to take up the responsibilities of acting director until a full-time director could be found. Mrs. Relf, also an active board member, helped her husband with the supervisory duties. Through the later part of the sixties, Mrs. Relf was also intimately involved with the Hope Mission's Sunday school.

The Relfs had compassion for people, particularly for the impoverished and the vulnerable. During their time as superintendents, they encountered a young man who had come from France. Someone at the single men's hostel had directed him to Hope Mission. The young Frenchman was in particular straits as he could neither read nor write. He made his way in life by stealing. Even so, something about his vulnerability tugged at the hearts of the Relfs, and they invited him to stay at their home, where they taught him rudimentary English. They also helped him find employment and encouraged him to look after himself without resorting to theft. No doubt it was because of their Christlike hospitality and concern that the young man was compelled to follow the same Lord that the Relfs followed.

In May 1971, the Relfs returned from their vacation and announced their resignation. The board members were taken by surprise. At the same time, light had already been shed on a probable reason for their resignation. Board members Mr. Hunt and Mr. Schlamp, who were filling in for the Relfs, found that the evening services were seriously and habitually interrupted by certain intoxicated men. As a remedy, two additional board members were recruited to bring order to the services. Soon there was "an entirely different spirit in the meetings and the Lord was working." It was then understood that the reason for the Relfs' retirement was quite likely burnout. Norman, with the sole help of his wife, had been in charge of evening services seven days a week with few breaks. They were no doubt exhausted and through the clarity of time away must have felt the ongoing situation called for their withdrawal.

It's unclear whether their resignation resulted from the stoic independence of the Relfs to forgo communicating their need for help or an assumption by the board along with a failure to occasionally observe the evening services. Whatever the case, there was a failure of communication that resulted in an avoidable rupture. Significantly, the board acknowledged the breakdown.

The board wrote the Relfs, accepting their resignation but with genuine regret. They also had a plaque made signifying their appreciation for the

Relfs' work at the Mission. At the following board meeting a discussion took place, stressing the need to monitor and put in place a supervision rotation that would give weekly relief for those responsible for the evening services. Although the Relfs moved on to rural ministry, they kept in contact with Hope Mission. On at least a couple of occasions Norman's love for the inner city brought him back to help out with evening services.

With the Relfs' resignation and the Hunts going on vacation, a letter with a plea for help was dispatched to Scotty McEwan. Scotty was living in Kelowna but had helped out by covering vacationing supervisors the previous year. Scotty was offered $150 per month. After Howard Hunt returned, Scotty was asked to stay on until the end of 1971, when he was asked to stay on as supervisor of men's ministry and as family counsellor. He was also invited to sit as a member of the board.

During the unsettled summer of 1971 the board had invited applications for superintendent. Several inquiries came in, but the one that most interested the board was from a well-known missionary. Manley Hodges had served for many years in Ethiopia and was now looking for a change and a new challenge. He was very interested in the work of Hope Mission, and as a man of charity and sincerity he would have offered strong and caring leadership to the Mission. It was, however, not to be. The Mission was still in debt and was barely able to meet its meagre payroll. And although the $350 per month Manley Hodges requested was clearly within reason, the board had to pass on the opportunity. To the delight of the board, eight months later Manley Hodges came to serve the Mission for two years as a board member.

HOWARD AND EILEEN HUNT

Howard Hunt and his wife, Eileen, came to Hope Mission under certain urgency but with thankful hearts. Howard arrived having hands-on experience in mission work through his employment at Turning Point. On one level, that ministry was one the Hunts no doubt would have liked to forget. Having invested and entrusted their livelihood to Turning Point, they turned around to find their trust violated and their money gone. They had lost everything in their venture. Despite this major blow, Howard and Eileen didn't abandon ministry. Howard was young, energetic and something of a visionary.

Howard Hunt brought with him, by permission of the disbanding board of Turning Point, chairs, desks, an electric range and other odds and ends. He was also given Turning Point's list of donors, a list that then became part of Hope Mission's contacts. Appropriately, Howard had taken time to inform these supporters of his new ministry and to ask their support for Hope Mission.

Howard came on staff in August 1970 as supervisor of Hope Mission's Sunday school. He soon began helping out in other areas of the Mission, and in the spring of 1971 he was brought on as Hope Mission's superintendent. Howard and Eileen, with their five children, moved into the manse that stood next to the church. Of their arrival at Hope Mission Eileen said, "There's no question we were led by God to

Hope Mission." She added, "We were young; we felt like children."

Howard and Eileen quickly immersed themselves in the ministry. Seeing a need, they restarted the afore-mentioned Sunday school for inner-city children. They soon found that the children who came were often hungry, so they began providing a lunch along with the program. Even while managing her household and raising her own children, Eileen was fully involved in children's Sunday school, from teaching to preparing lunches.

Howard had a broad vision that helped solidify Hope Mission's position in the community. He had no desire to see Hope Mission operating as an island, and he did his best to publicize the work of the Mission to the Christian community and the community at large. He worked hard to involve other Christians in serving the inner city. He was a good administrator and believed in what he was doing. During his leadership he had as many as 100 volunteers working together to put on fourteen separate services or events per week. During any given week as many as 700 people were helped and in some way cared for through the various services.

It has been said that if every Christian family would adopt one poor person, there wouldn't be enough poor people to go around. On a local level this is surely true, but it was Howard's plan to test the theory and see what happened. He used the Mission's newsletter to suggest that able Christian families adopt an inner-city family. He wasn't necessarily surprised when after sev-eral weeks he hadn't received a response. But then

Howard got a letter. It was from a Mrs. McIntyre, joyfully sharing that in response to his suggestion she had indeed adopted an inner-city family. She had already visited the home and looked forward to becoming a family friend. She closed her letter saying that she was now preparing gifts for each of the children for her return visit.

In June 1973, Howard and Eileen resigned. Herb Jamieson, chairman at the time, tried to have Howard reconsider, but without success. The Hunts simply felt that it was the right time to leave. It was a decision based primarily on the needs of their large and growing family. There was also, with justification, a sense of accomplishment about what they had been able to bring to the Mission. They were a key part of bringing Hope Mission through its second major transition.

In the ensuing Hope Mission newsletter Herb Jamieson wrote, "The past three years since our move into our present quarters have been like a miracle to us. Mr. and Mrs. Hunt are greatly responsible. We can hardly conceive of coming so far without them."

Reciprocally, the Mission provided Eileen and Howard with a time and place for vocational and personal transition. Today Eileen still talks passionately about their time at Hope Mission. She said, "We saw many miracles while we were there. Even our going there was like a miracle. God brought us to Hope Mission at just the right time."

John (Scotty) McEwan

During the early part of the Hunts' ministry the couple met and worked closely with Scotty McEwen.

Eileen Hunt explained, "He was a ray of sunshine. He just showed up at the door one day and was an incredible help to us."

John McEwan Scotty, as he came to be known came to volunteer at Hope Mission sometime in 1966. His earlier history is less clear. By one accounting, Scotty was found by Harold Edwardson on the doorstep of the first Mission. Scotty was a broke, suicidal alcoholic at the end of his tether. He was taken in by Hope Mission, and after experiencing a reception of love, he gave himself over to Jesus Christ. In getting his life back, he never forgot Hope Mission, and years later he came back to volunteer.

Scotty McEwan was an energetic and enigmatic Scotsman with a wonderfully heavy accent. And he loved to preach. Over the years he was afforded ample opportunity to do just this and became well known both inside and outside of Hope Mission. Although Scotty preferred preaching, he didn't shirk the other forms of mission work. In fact, he became a kind of general practitioner of the Mission.

Scotty came to hold a supervisory position as well as a position on the board of directors. Herb Jamieson explained, "He just kind of grew into it." Herb also believed that it was because of Scotty's "plain zeal" that the Mission maintained itself through uncertain times in the late sixties and early seventies. Some of the Mission's support was falling off simply through the attrition of original benefactors. With the coming and going of superintendents, Scotty was there to fill the gaps. As Herb Jamieson recalled, "Scotty kept it open, which for that time is saying a lot." Herb added, "He used to find great quantities of bread, and he made sure the Mission kept providing a lunch every night."

Scotty's zeal was evident in all areas of the Mission. He was not shy to speak his mind with emotion and passion—even to directors on the board. At a June meeting in 1972, in the way that only Scotty could, he shared the despair in his heart over what he felt was the "slackness of spiritual interest shown on behalf of the board members in regards to the daily work of the Mission." He gave allowance for the general busyness of all the members, but he felt that part of the responsibility of serving Hope Mission as a board member was to be present, at least occasionally, during an evening service or a prayer meeting. For Scotty, even if a perennial absence didn't truly reflect a member's indifference for the Mission, it nevertheless communicated a lack of concern. Scotty explained that his burden was not so much for staff but for those the Mission served—that they would know the extent to which the entire Mission cared about them.

No doubt, there was more energy at this meeting than usual. Scotty had expressed what for him needed expressing, and it had good effect. Chairman Harold Burma thanked Scotty for his "great concern" and assured him that "a greater effort would be put forth by the Board as a whole in supporting the staff by attendance now and again, and by prayer support." Scotty then left the meeting, but not before praying for each of the board members and for the Mission.

Long-time volunteer Maynard Cole said about Scotty McEwan, "He wasn't very big, in fact he was shorter than me, but he was all there. And he could sure play the banjo." Maynard added, "But he was a soul winner, a real soul winner of the streets, kind of like Kevin Roland and Darcy Godin."

Darcy Godin and Kevin Roland were what could be termed street chaplains. Both Darcy and Kevin are gifted in unique and varied ways. They both fit and held a variety of positions within Hope Mission, primarily through the 1990s. But their real love was being "on the street," being with the people in their environment. Whether it was in the taverns, in the parks or on the sidewalk, they were at home and had an effortless easygoing way of showing compassion and creating opportunities to talk about Jesus.

In 1974, when the Mission had a new full-time director, Scotty McEwan resigned. But he couldn't resign from ministry. He stayed in the inner city and on the street, ministering to his "friends," as he always called them.

Scotty did have a streak of self-direction, and after leaving Hope Mission he tried to open up his own street mission, close to the Salvation Army hostel. There is however no record of whether he was successful. Although Scotty McEwan served Hope Mission in many capacities, he felt his role most keenly as a minister and servant to the inner city. In this way he was a blessing to the Mission, but more, he was God's instrument of hope for the less fortunate and forgotten ones. These he kept easy company with because he loved them and knew them from the inside.

Lilly Lewis

In the fall of 1969 Mrs. Lilly Lewis took over supervising Hope Mission's Sunday school program. In a report written in January 1970, she described the tone of Hope Mission's Sunday school program. "The presence of God is so real in our humble little place of worship that we cannot help but shout for joy and give thanks." Shouting for joy and giving thanks are actions that define Lilly. She is a pearl that the pressures of an arduous life helped create.

Lilly Lewis grew up in the Provost area of Alberta. Lilly and her twin were the youngest in a large family. Her family, like many pioneer families, experienced the poverty and hardships of the time. When the Second World War broke out, Lilly signed on and served in an administrative role in the Royal Canadian Air Force. After the war, she returned home and married. She had four children, but not long after her youngest child was born, her husband became ill. After a long fight with cancer he died. Lilly never remarried.

As a young single mother, Lilly moved with her children to Edmonton. Although she arrived with nothing, she refused to go on welfare. She was, however, not without resources. Stenographer skills she learned while in the air force were put to use as she became the personal secretary to a series of provincial cabinet ministers. But being on her own and with the financial demands of a growing family, she also had to work evenings and weekends. Lilly was often away from her children, but one thing was kept sacred. Daily she would gather her family and have devotions, and as she did, she would pray and entrust each of her children to God. Early in their lives the children took on responsibilities and began to earn their own way.

Mrs. Melsness, a friend of Lilly's, wrote, "I have often marvelled how Lil could pack so much activity into a 24-hour day. On Sunday mornings she would take the sermons in shorthand, and then share them with her family and friends. She rarely missed the weekly Bible Study and Prayer. Her well-worn Bible goes with her wherever she goes. She witnesses wherever she goes."

Lilly's life was full, but she still experienced a kind of restlessness. It was, she sensed, the restlessness of a yet indefinite inner calling. She often wondered whether God wanted her to go into foreign missions. She desired this direction, but the opportunity always seemed closed to her. Then she found out about Hope Mission through a volunteer in her church. Lilly saw this as a substantial answer to her desire for mission work, and she began helping out at the Mission's Sunday school programs.

Lilly's versatility and capacity for work soon had her supervising the Sunday school programs. A few months after she came to the Mission, she was invited onto the board of directors. Lilly loved to work with the inner-city children. Besides the weekly programs, she helped to organize and teach at Hope Mission's daily vacation bible school and at the summer camps. She involved herself in most anything that needed doing. At the Mission all kinds of people gravitated to Lilly because she cared and was a tireless listener. In Lily's typical fashion, along with everything else she was involved in she began studies to help her become a more capable counsellor.

Lily Lewis resigned from Hope Mission in September 1974. Not long after, she went to Nepal to work at the

Canadian consulate. There, in her heart and by her actions, she was able to be the overseas missionary she had dreamed about. Over the five years that Lilly volunteered at Hope Mission her joy, innate energy and closeness to God drew many young lives to Christ.

RESURGENCE

Under the guidance of the Relfs, the Hunts and Scotty McEwan and through the industry of people like Lilly Lewis, Hope Mission's latest facility came to life.

Part of the life and new energy at the Mission was the result of an informal partnership with Youth for Christ. A number of youth rallies were held, and the initiative spawned a weekly coffee gathering called the Catacomb Coffee House. It was held in the basement of the Mission. The coffee house became a significant outreach to the youth of the inner city and beyond. As part of a joint youth ministry effort, the cottage that stood behind the church was rented out to Bible college students. The student leaders also helped out the Mission in other ways and worked off part of their rent by cleaning the Mission.

The Sunday school outreach program also experienced a resurgence. The simple two-part program consisted of basic Bible lessons and Sunday morning worship, with a time in the afternoon for activities and games. The afternoon component, called Children's Hour, concluded with a hot lunch for all. According to the 1972 annual report, the Sunday school program grew from an average attendance of a mere handful to more than 100. At the program's height, the Mission leased two buses to bring the children to the programs.

As well, Daily Vacation Bible School (DVBS) grew out of the Sunday school program. This was due to the supervision and hard work of Lilly Lewis and others. Because of the children, natural connections were made with parents, and as a result an adult Sunday school class was started. At times there were more than thirty adults, mostly parents, coming to the classes.

According to additional reports, the women's program was the avenue for what Scotty McEwan would refer to as "a great harvest of souls." The women's meetings were held every Tuesday afternoon. Tea was served, clothing was distributed, and many other practical needs were addressed. All who came were cared for. It was also a time when the women could hear the gospel. On a number of occasions, Sister Glubish a volunteer would translate the gospel message into the Cree language, since there were a significant number of native women. In one meeting of fifty-two ladies, twenty-five went forward to "pray and give their lives to Christ." One report stated that the impact of this was felt throughout the community as many of these women "continued to witness of it afterward."

The Mission's church facility was constantly active, and the ministry of the Mission was thriving. While the sanctuary on the main floor of the Mission was booked for conferences, used as a meeting place for other agencies and sometimes for weddings, funerals and other functions, the evening services in the basement—still the generative hub of the Mission—flourished. Average attendance for these services was around 100 with as many as 170 attending on occasion. Through all these efforts, to the delight of Hope

Mission's leaders, men, women, youth and children were responding to the call and message of Jesus Christ. A number of truncated notations in the board minutes reflect this reality. One such entry simply states, "Mrs. Poundmaker has had a tremendous experience in meeting the Lord."

RAY BUTTERY

Ray Buttery could never escape the idea that the gospel demanded a practical response. His concern for the underprivileged grew through this conviction, which finally brought him to Hope Mission. Ray started by attending Sunday evening services and volunteering to serve sandwiches and clean up the Mission after the services. He became a member of the society in February 1972. His sincerity and dedication soon earned him an invitation onto the board of directors, yet the added obligation never prevented him from continuing his hands-on work at the Mission. With his sons, he routinely did the "pickups" of donated food and clothing for the Mission. Then, with any other spare time he found, he put his background in carpentry to use in repairing and remodelling the Mission facility. It was work that was ongoing and much needed.

During the months after Howard Hunt's resignation, Ray became increasingly absorbed by the idea of applying for the supervisory position. He finally did, and with the board's due consideration, his application was accepted. Ray resigned his teaching position in the vocational department at L.Y. Cairns School and stepped into the role of supervisor in the fall of 1973.

A central desire of the Mission was that it be seen as a practical arm of the local church but that it not be used as a platform for any single denomination. With the growth of the evening gospel service, more churches came on board, bringing their own unique programs, which provided richness. However, with a few churches emphasizing peripheral doctrinal stands, it became increasingly difficult to monitor and maintain a desirable distance from denominational characteristics. Recognizing this, Ray Buttery decided on his first task to draw up a statement of faith that would help maintain the simple basis of the gospel message. He then drew up policy and a standard of practice that gave guidance to volunteer evangelists and Christian workers. According to Ray, this effort proved itself in evangelical churches downplaying their various denominational traits while working in greater unison for the sake of the gospel.

Ray also carried on the weekly afternoon meeting for women. It was a special time for women to connect, which resulted in mutual support. As noted, the meeting combined a gospel message with food and clothing distribution. Since there was interest and goodwill in the larger community for this meeting and ministry, donations came in. While the food came from individual donors and stores like Safeway, the clothes freely came from individuals and occasionally from stores such as Woodward's. Ray explained, "For a time, a small cost was levied to discourage freeloading, as some would sell the goods to thrift stores." Most importantly, single women, mothers and women on welfare were always helped.

Over the years, Hope Mission has been able to distribute food and clothing through the goodwill of people and businesses. The Mission has been blessed to be able to be a kind of clearinghouse for the service of Edmonton's poor. Of course to do this effectively and responsibly requires a great deal of effort; it also requires a simple and efficient administrative system. Throughout the life of Hope Mission, both staff and volunteers have pitched in to make this an ongoing part of their ministry.

Ray Buttery also carried on the children's Sunday school outreach that Howard and Eileen Hunt had started. Before long he had requests from various parts of the city to pick up children. He arranged for them to be picked up by car, but the demand soon forced the Mission to purchase two second-hand school buses. Volunteer drivers were found, and occasionally the teachers would help out. Ray said, "There was often a full house, over a hundred kids...the kids, many of whom were native, were often very hungry."

Because of the need and the success of the ministry, Ray Buttery turned his attention to creating a boys' and a girls' club. The kids, mostly from the Sunday school outreach, were bused in, girls on Tuesdays and boys on Fridays. Those over twelve years old came on Saturday evening. Attendance ran as high as seventy at the boys' club. A point system was set up for attendance, memorizing Bible verses and other endeavours. They played games and sang choruses, and later there was always an object lesson. Ray reflected that "this involved a lot of work and organization, but it was worth the evident spiritual fruit."

Hope Mission had occasionally published a newsletter in an effort to make known the work of the Mission to interested individuals and churches. However, Ray established a monthly newsletter, publishing testimonials, pictures, articles and news of needs and events. With keen deliberation, he used the newsletter to create interest in Hope Mission's ministries and to generate sponsorship for children's summer camps.

SUMMER CAMP

Until the summer of 1972, Hope Mission had not run its own summer camp program. The children they cared for were referred to other camps. Through the diligence of volunteers like Lily Lewis, Miss Windom and Mrs. Relf, inner-city children were often sponsored or given consideration because of their ties with Hope Mission. Starting in the late sixties these children were transported to camps at Ross Haven, Nakamun and Rocky Mountain House. Hope Mission workers would also volunteer at these camps. This was appreciated by the regular camp staff, but more importantly it provided the inner-city children with support through the comfort of familiar faces.

In February 1972, a delegation from the Ottwell Christian Reform Church offered a Stony Hill farm site to Hope Mission to develop a summer camp program. That summer they borrowed a number of tents, gathered a small staff of cooks and counsellors, and set up Hope Mission's first summer camp for underprivileged kids. Two camps were held that first summer. Nineteen girls attended the first one, and ten boys came to the second camp. Almost all were there because of their association with the Sunday school program.

The camp's financial needs were met through donations and gifts. Quite unexpectedly, at the end of camp there was even a balance on hand of 150 dollars. There were logistical problems, but as Ray Buttery put it, "What made the effort worthwhile was the fact that three girls asked the Lord Jesus to come into their hearts."

The problems encountered were not enough to dampen the desire to do it again. The following year the Mission again used the Stony Hill farm. However, the arrangement could not be sustained; the camp was growing and needed extra space.

In the summer of 1974 Hope Mission made some inquiries and was granted the use of a government owned campground near Sundre. Then, in 1975, the Mission was offered a farm near Sherwood Park, close to the Stony Hill farm. There was more space to set up the tents, and there was also a cottage that was used for mealtimes and Bible teaching. Ray wrote,

> It was a wet and miserable summer, but we managed to achieve our spiritual goals. In total 58 girls and boys went to camp. The kids were individually sponsored and at the end of camp each child was asked to take time to write and thank their sponsors. It was disclosed through the letters that 20 kids received Christ in their lives.

In 1976, Hope Mission acquired a ninety-nine-year government lease for Crown land on the shores of Joseph Lake, east of Edmonton. They began to build their own camp. In the Mission's ever-present spirit of "making do," the old parsonage that stood beside the Mission in the city was salvaged, and the lumber went toward building the camp. A long ranch-style building that housed the kitchen and dinning area was also constructed. The facility also doubled as a chapel and a meeting area. The cabins that had been built on the first farm were moved and upgraded. Areas for softball, broomball and tetherball were cleared and the entire camp landscaped. A great deal of work went into this effort.

Ray Buttery recalled the summer camps at Joseph Lake with fondness. "The meals were wonderful and the kids, many of whom suffered from some kind of neglect and abuse, had a great time. There was a real spirit of co-operation and sacrifice among the staff."

The summer of 1979 saw two new cabins built at Joseph Lake and an amalgamation with Native Christian Fellowship, a native Christian mission group from Hobbema. A joint venture was only natural, because over 75 percent of the kids attending the camps were native. Under this new co-operative arrangement the camp was officially named the Hope Mission Beaver Bible Camp.

In 1980, under Ed Enarson and Hope Mission's revised direction and policy change, the Native Christian Fellowship was given exclusive use of the camp. The Native Christian Fellowship was doing very good work, and they had over 200 native children attend their first camp. The Native Christian Fellowship subsequently took over the Joseph Lake lease, and Hope Mission's camping program ended.

WILLIAM NISH, HANK VELEMA, W.O. BOOKER

There are many who have influenced the direction and the culture of Hope Mission simply through quiet service and hard work. William Nish became involved with Hope Mission in 1959. He served tirelessly and efficiently as a board member and secretary and then as chairman in 1979. After Ray Buttery resigned, William was called upon to step into the superintendent's role until Hope Mission was able to find a full-time director. William (Bill) Nish is described as a gentle and kind man, a man who truly cared about and loved people. He was also an able preacher. Bill served the Mission as director for just over a year. He was assisted for a time by Hank Velema.

Hank Velema started helping out in 1974 with camp work. Hank, also known as "the big Dutchman," was extremely helpful in various construction projects, renovations and landscaping work. He joined the Mission board in late 1974 and served into the early 1980s. Hank and his wife also helped with the evening services for several years. He lent a hand where he could, but he was especially valuable in overseeing building and maintenance projects. Hank Velema also proved himself as a diplomat. During the early stages of Hope Mission's camping initiative, through a regrettable misunderstanding, the Mission's cabins and some equipment were seized. It was through Hank's handling of this imbroglio that the Mission's property was eventually released. This property finally found its way to the Joseph Lake camp, where Hank's involvement also proved vital.

W.O. Booker moved through the Mission, always

with a word of encouragement and an easy smile. As a board member, he began serving Hope Mission in the mid 1960s and stayed for almost twenty years. During much of that time he served as treasurer. Booker, as he was known, was from southern Texas and had the heavy drawl to prove it. Herb Jamieson said, "For a long time I thought we called him Booker because he always did the books." Herb remembers him as a "godly man with unique style." But what impressed Herb and the board more than anything about W.O. Booker was his confidence that Hope Mission was God's mission and God would see it through. Booker was with the Mission during some of its most vulnerable days, and during those times he instilled the board with much needed confidence through his own unwavering belief. That Booker was also the treasurer through some of those sparse times only added to his infectious and simple assurance.

THE FIRE

On the night of the fire it was windy, rainy and cold. The Mission had always tried to prevent or at least discourage street people from congregating under the steps of the old church building, but this night the weather encouraged some not only to seek its shelter but also to start a fire to keep the chill off. It wasn't the first time a fire was started under these steps, however this time carelessness and wind carried the flames up into the dry wood underside of the stairway. The fire spread quickly, but fortunately the wind that fanned it also blew it away from the main building. The fire department arrived in six minutes and got the blaze under control and finally extinguished.

This was remarkable considering the old building's conditions. There was considerable damage to the front entrance, and the basement of the church, where all the evening services were held, was flooded with water. Prudently, two years earlier the board of Hope Mission had examined its fire insurance policy and decided to improve the Mission's protection. Apart from Hope Mission's desire to continue the nightly evening services, it might have been a blessing if the entire structure had burned down because it *was* such a fire hazard. Nevertheless, the Mission collected close to $30,000 fire insurance.

There was some interruption of services as water in the basement was pumped out and repairs were done. Renovations were rudimentary though since the Mission was now on an "as needed" maintenance schedule. The building was already over seventy-five years old and even without fire damage was not worth refurbishing.

In the ensuing months, the now decrepit cottage, which stood on the second lot, was torn down. The lot was rented first to a used car dealer and then to the school board for parking. The resulting income helped cover some of the utility bills. But general operating costs remained a concern. This, coupled with the increasing difficulty of running a ministry out of a decrepit building, placed the Mission at yet another crossroads.

Setting a Course:
Change and Stability

Unless the Lord builds the house, those who build it labor in vain. Unless the Lord guards the city, the guard keeps watch in vain (Psalm 127:1).

REV. ED ENARSON

In 1942, Ed Enarson went to war. Conscription was not something he hoped for, but when the letter came, Ed enlisted. He had graduated from missionary medical school and before that from Prairie Bible School. He could have been ordained, as several of his colleagues had been, thus averting the draft. Ed's conscience wouldn't allow this, so he served overseas with the Canadian New Westminster Regiment as first aid detachment commander. Four years later he was awarded the military medal for service beyond the call of duty.

After Ed's discharge from the army in 1947, he went to Nigeria with Sudan Interior Mission. There he met his wife, Shirley McCreary. After getting married in 1949 and learning the Hausa language, they were assigned to train native Nigerians as Bible school teachers, evangelists and pastors.

After Nigeria received its independence in 1960, the Enarsons returned to Canada. For the next fifteen years Ed and Shirley ministered in several evangelical churches.

In April 1978, Ed Enarson received a call from Herb Jamieson inviting him to become the director of Hope Mission. Herb had known Ed for many years, but it was former premier Harry Strom who brought Ed's name forward for consideration as director. Harry and Ed Enarson attended the same Evangelical Free church. Ed's first response was "I don't know anything about running a mission."

Herb countered, "You've been a pastor and a missionary...I think that gives you lots of qualifications." Ed agreed to consider the invitation and told Herb he would give him an answer in one month. In May 1978, Ed Enarson took the over the reins of the Mission.

CHANGE OF FOCUS

Ed Enarson describes his time as director of the Mission as years of change. He had a clear idea of what a rescue mission's mandate should be, and from his first day he set out with a disciplined determination to bring about the change. He believed, perhaps with more intensity than those before him, that a mission should be first and foremost an arm of the established churches. Ed thought that Hope Mission had "become another church," and because of this he felt it was hurting itself and in some respects hurting the local churches as well. Ed saw this as a sort of Catch-22. The churches didn't have full use of the arm, because the arm wanted to be the body. And because the churches didn't make use of Hope

Mission, the Mission in some ways defaulted towards becoming church-like.

Ed Enarson was in no way against the Sunday school or camp programs, but he believed that these were more properly initiatives of the churches and as such should be run by the churches. Seeing the need, the Mission had developed these programs in good faith and with good results. However, Ed's vision was to build close ties with the local churches. He believed the churches would rightfully take over the programs as those ties developed. One initiative he put forward to allow churches a sense of ownership was to institute voting privileges for churches that regularly supported Hope Mission. Any church that donated $50 or more per month would be able to have a voice in the direction and operation of Hope Mission.

A primary passion of Ed Enarson's was to see the churches take legitimate ownership of caring for the poor. As an arm of the churches, Hope Mission was the churches' place of contact with Edmonton's poor. Ed was troubled about the practice of churches that came and shared the gospel, as he put it, "without any responsibility to become further involved with those who responded to the message of salvation." It became Ed's fervent request of those who represented a local church that they take an active part in following up on people who responded in their services and try to integrate them in their own church fellowships. By this, Rev. Enarson was also recognizing that Christian love must extend itself beyond a desire to save souls.

Native Crusade

One of Ed Enarson's inspirations as he pondered the overrepresentation of native people in the inner city was to plan an evangelistic crusade for aboriginals. He felt an outreach event like this could be a much-needed energizing force for the overall ministry to Edmonton's native population. The result of his efforts was that in the fall of 1979, after a year of planning and committee meetings, Hope Mission and twenty-three evangelical churches banded together to sponsor the first and possibly most successful native evangelistic crusade in the city of Edmonton.

A significant part of this success was because Ed was able to contact First Nations evangelist Chief Ken Antone, an Oneida Indian who grew up in London, Ontario. Ken, an ordained Baptist minister, and his musically gifted family made their life's calling "missionary evangelism" to native peoples. By the time the Antones came to Edmonton their ministry was already well established across North America. Their method was to seek out small reservations and native communities that didn't have a church and hadn't been exposed to the gospel. Their giftedness preceded them, and they occasionally found themselves performing at such venues as the 1976 Olympic games and the Grand Ole Opry, where they received a standing ovation. But their true calling remained to the native people, and the campaign in Edmonton was the kind of ministry possibility that captured their hearts.

Through prayer and planning the crusade was a catalyst to renewed ministry to the aboriginal population of Edmonton. Harvey Town, pastor of Beulah Alliance Church and co-chair of the crusade, reported that sixty-five men and women gave their lives to Christ during the week-long event.

Two aboriginal churches emerged from the native crusade. One church met at Beulah Alliance under their supervision, and the other met at Hope Mission under the care of Interact Missions, formerly Arctic Missions. The Mission's Sunday school, which at the time was primarily attended by native children, was reorganized. Many of these children had been bused in from other parts of Edmonton, and efforts were now made to have neighbourhood churches welcome these children into their own congregations. At the same time the children from the inner city were now able to attend their own church. Ed Enarson delighted to see the local church meeting the local need.

THE MISSION TURNS FIFTY

Ed Enarson was an idealist, but it was just such idealism that brought new stability to the Mission. Having refocused the work of Hope Mission, Ed expressed his concern to the board that a new facility was needed. This was a shared concern. Herb Jamieson and Harry Strom had already recognized the need, and one reason Ed was recruited was because they felt his resolve and tenacity were just what was required to take the Mission through a building project if the board decided to go that direction.

Ed Enarson had taken the liberty of using the old Mission to house the occasional street person with special needs. But these were makeshift and temporary efforts. What Ed envisioned was a building that could be built specifically for rescue mission work. Ed's catch phrase for this initiative was "redemptive rehabilitation." He envisioned the new facility as housing men, particularly those who had desire to change and were seeking rehabilitation. The building would need adequate space for chapel meetings and banquets and a proper kitchen area.

In the beginning of 1979 the Mission was free and clear of all debt except the loan repayment of $10,000 to Martha Pehl. Financially the Mission was in better shape than it had been in a long time. The board was faced with a critical decision. The option of continuing as they were was effectively closed off. The derelict and mouse-ridden old church was probably already past being condemned. Looking for another location with an existing facility was a possibility, but they already had property in a good location.

At a historic board meeting, after much prayer and discussion, a vote was taken on whether to go ahead with a building project. It passed. To not go ahead spelled the possible demise of the Mission or at the very best a step backwards.

The following morning Ed received a phone call from board member Harry Strom. Harry was unable to sleep that night. He had had misgivings and felt they needed to call another meeting and reconsider. He was concerned about the timing of the project. Ed told Harry that they had decided in good faith and needed to carry through with the decision. Ed added, "I'd sooner have God close the Mission than us." Harry accepted this wisdom, and the board began to make plans for fundraising. Harry Strom and Herb Jamieson co-chaired the building committee.

The coming of Hope Mission's 50th anniversary was great motivation for the board to embark on the most ambitious project in the history of the Mission. In October 1979, Hope Mission held its 50th anniversary banquet at Beulah Alliance Church. There the Mission officially announced, "After months of prayer and deliberation, the board has moved to establish a building fund in this year of our jubilee." Ed Enarson borrowed a fundraising slogan from Sudan Interior Mission: "Full information without pressured solicitation." With this, the Mission launched what he called "an aggressive building program." At the banquet the Mission received close to $17,000 in cash and pledges.

Ed Enarson, Harry Strom, Herb Jamieson and the board began to beat the financial "bushes." Herb went to every lending institution in the city. "Most laughed because we were a mission, no membership, no collateral," he recalled. "But the Bank of Montreal finally decided to take us on and underwrite us. However, we [the board members] all needed to agree to sign promissory notes of $3,000 or more." It was a board decision, and everybody pitched in.

Ed Enarson remembered the months of campaigning for funds with Harry Strom as "exciting and satisfying. We spoke in churches when and where we could—we made dozens of personal visits." Ed remembered the day he and Harry met Mrs. Belle Pahl for tea. Roland Pahl, Belle's husband, had owned a car dealership and had passed away some time earlier. The Pahls were acquainted with the Edwardsons and knew something about Hope Mission, so it wasn't a cold call.

The conversation eventually turned to the Mission's building project, and Ed asked whether Belle might be willing to contribute. She thought for a moment and recited a figure. Then she added, "But you'll need another $5,000 for the organ; your chapel will need an organ." Belle continued, "Do you think this is enough, or should I add some more?"

Ed laughed and said, "Belle, you can keep adding all you want!" Ed and Harry left with a cheque for $80,000.

Some donations just walked in through the door. One blustery day an ill-dressed man came into the Mission and asked to see Mr. Enarson. He told Ed that he had read the article in the *Edmonton Journal* about Hope Mission's building project and had come to drop off a cheque. He thanked Ed for the work Hope Mission was doing, placed a cheque face down on the desk and left. Ed looked at the back of the cheque and thought, "Wouldn't it be nice if it was $500?" He turned it over, revealing the figure of $10,000. Through both ordinary and seemingly remarkable ways, God consistently provided for Hope Mission's new building.

Ed retired from Hope Mission in 1986, but he and his wife, Shirley, continued to be active in the church for many years. Two years into his tenure as director, Ed had written, "I have been in service for my Lord for forty years, and in all that time, nowhere have I witnessed greater dedication and faithfulness in the work of the Lord than here at the Mission." He also credited his wife, Shirley, for the success of his ministry at Hope

Mission. In accepting his call to Hope Mission he said, "I never made salary a deciding factor when I was called to the Mission; it was because of my wife's work and ministry at Cornerstone that I was able to carry on my work here." Toward the end of Ed's tenure, Shirley also volunteered as his personal secretary, which for Ed "was invaluable."

Ed Enarson was born on June 14, 1919, and died June 30, 2001. His was a rich and varied life of service. In his own inimitable way, only a few months before he died, Ed described his legacy with Hope Mission as "a three-stage affair—the mouse stage, the mortar stage and the men stage." He recalled with a smile, "Martha Pehl and me caught and hauled out as many as a dozen mice per day out of the old Mission. I was so thankful for the new building and the new ministry opportunity that it gave us. The building's design and purpose, after all, is simply to help us reach the men in the inner city."

HARRY STROM

Harry E. Strom joined Hope Mission's board of directors a few years after he lost his bid to be elected in the 1971 provincial election.   Born on July 7, 1914, in Burdett, Alberta, Harry Strom had the distinction of being the first premier of Alberta who was actually born in the province. In October 1938, he married Ruth Johnson of Bow Island and started a family. They eventually had six children. In addition to farming, Harry was always active in community affairs. He was unassuming and soft-spoken and never really sought a political life. He simply agreed to have his name stand because his neighbours asked him to run as councillor. In 1941, he was elected councillor for the municipal district of Forty Mile.

Harry Strom ran and was elected as the Social Credit candidate for the electoral district of Cypress at the provincial general election of June 29, 1955. He was re-elected in 1959, 1963, 1967 and 1971. Between 1962 and 1968, he served as minister of agriculture, and in 1967, he was appointed the first chairman of the Alberta Human Resources Authority. During the last six months of 1968, he served as minister of municipal affairs.

In 1967, Premier Ernest C. Manning resigned as leader of the Alberta Social Credit Party. In December 1968, at the subsequent Social Credit convention, Harry was elected as leader, and on December 12, 1968, he was appointed premier of Alberta by Lieutenant-Governor Grant MacEwan.

During Harry E. Strom's term as premier, the provincial government of Alberta took several social and environmental initiatives. Notably, in 1970, the Alberta Alcoholism and Drug Abuse Commission and the Environment Conservation Authority were established. In 1971, a new department of health and social development was organized. And that same year, ahead of the popular wave, Canada's first department of the environment was created.

In the provincial general election of 1971, Alberta's Social Credit government was defeated. Harry E. Strom, who had been re-elected in his riding, resigned as premier on September 10, 1971, and subsequently served as leader of the official opposition in the Alberta legislature from 1971 to 1973. He then resigned as leader of the Social Credit Party. In 1975, he left politics and returned to farming and his work with the Evangelical Free Church.

As well, Harry was a member of local school boards and the development board. In addition to this he held the positions of director of Rural Electrification Association, president of Burdett Home and School Association, president of Burdett Agricultural Improvement Association, member of the Southern Alberta Water Conservation Association, and director of Western Canada Reclamation Association.

As well as his numerous community activities, he was involved in his church. Until 1962, his family attended the Evangelical Free Church in Bow Island, where he served at various times as a Sunday school teacher, deacon and church chairman. He also held the office of chairman of the Evangelical Free Church of Canada. One of his deep commitments was to the Overseas Missions Board of the Evangelical Free Church of America; he served them for twenty-one years.

Harry Strom's social conscience had exposed him to the work of Hope Mission. Now, after politics, he was drawn to devote much of his time to the ministry of the Mission. At Hope Mission's annual general meeting on March 29, 1976, Harry Strom was elected onto the board of Hope Mission. He served as a board member and helped out in other areas where and when he could. Maynard Cole, a long-term Mission volunteer, remembered working alongside the former premier. They were cleaning and refurbishing the camp at Joseph Lake to prepare it for the summer camping season. Maynard noticed—almost with surprise, given the prestige of the office Mr. Strom once held—that "He worked hard and got dirty!"

Harry Strom was appointed chairman of Hope Mission's building committee in January 1979. Here Harry Strom's presence proved invaluable for the Mission. He led the inquiries and guided the process. His expertise, to a great extent, made possible the existence of a facility that would not only have the capacity to provide gospel services and meals for the people of the street, but also have rooms to shelter the homeless as well as having a residential program for those caught up in addictions.

"City's Downtrodden to Get New Hope"

Harry Strom would never allow himself to be seen as integral to the successful continuance of the Mission, yet he was. Ed Enarson believed that he was a friend in a high place that God providentially brought to the Mission at just the right time. His connections and, more importantly, his character and reputation allowed him easy access to people in government, both provincially and municipally. During such meetings, whether with Premier Peter Lougheed or Edmonton's mayor Cec Purves, his concern was to be an ambassador of the ministry of Hope Mission.

Mr. Strom had both the ability and credibility to help government officials—namely social services minister Bob Bogle—see how Hope Mission, over many years, served the very constituency that social services were concerned about. At a meeting with the ministers of social services, Harry Strom and Herb Jamieson—who also had political experience and was respected within governmental circles—proposed that Hope Mission's long and faithful service might now warrant some government beneficence. They also pointed out that for those past fifty years the Mission had not received any government assistance.

In an *Edmonton Journal* article Bob Bogle said he was impressed by the devoted work of Hope Mission volunteers. As a result the provincial government agreed to a special grant of up to $400,000, matching the dollars Hope Mission raised privately. In a follow-up newspaper article a spokesman for the Social Services Department said, "The department does not normally provide capital grants of this nature, but the Mission's role in supplementing government hostel programs merited special consideration."

On September 20, 1982, the ground-breaking ceremony for the *new* Hope Mission was held. The observance had an original and fitting connection—Mrs. Hillie Edwardson was invited to be the guest of honour. With great pride and satisfaction, Mrs. Edwardson, along with Harry Strom and Social Services Minister Bob Bogle, held the commemorative spade and turned the sod, ceremoniously commencing the construction of the Mission's new facility.

George Dochuk

Mr. George Dochuk, at the time a newer board member, was point man for the construction of the new facility. George had extensive knowledge of the industry but wanted the added experience of construction manager of a major building project. With the board's approval he volunteered himself as overseer. George produced the blueprints, began subcontracting and scheduling the various trades, and generally threw himself into the effort. But construction of Hope Mission's new facility was not without obstacles.

The winter of 1982–83 was snowy, bitter and cold. As with any project of this size, there were extra expenses. For the most part they were manageable, but compounded by the costs of trying to work through a harsh winter, they escalated. Nevertheless, through dogged determination, costly self-sacrifice and arduous work, George Dochuk prevailed.

By the spring of 1983 the building was closed in and completion in sight. Not satisfied, George Dochuk took it upon himself to visit a wide circle of churches in an effort to raise funds and donations for furnishing the new Mission. The final cost of the furnished facility slightly eclipsed one million dollars. The mortgage on the added expense was burned several years later. Herb Jamieson stated, "If there's one name that deserves to be on that building, it's George's."

DEDICATION

Hillie Edwardson gave a brief impromptu speech at the dedication and open house of Hope Mission's new facility. With obvious emotion she gave thanks, recounting God's long-term care of Hope Mission. It was September 25, 1983, fifty-four years after Hillie and her husband first opened the Mission doors. Hillie Edwardson died just six weeks later. She was eighty-six.

Harry Strom, who had laboured hard from concept to completion, was also at the dedication. As part of the ceremony Harry received the keys from George

Dochuk and presented the chapel plaque. A year later, on October 2, 1984, Harry Strom died of cancer. He was buried in the Chapel Lawn Cemetery at Medicine Hat, Alberta.

The completion of the new facility was a milestone for Hope Mission. It represented more than a new lease on the Mission's life and ministry. It was one more sign of God's faithfulness—as discovered in the acts of communal faith by the leaders of Hope Mission. The team effort of faith and diligence by the board of directors plus the hard work, attention to detail and general changes brought about by Director Ed Enarson gained the Mission renewed stability and a foundation that well positioned it for future growth.

**Mr. and Mrs. Edwardson in front of the
First Mission**

**1930s Mission staff and families with the
Edwardson children in the foreground**

Dagmar Cunningham (Edwardson)

**Hope Mission on 101 Street. A young Paul
Edwardson in the Mission's delivery truck**

Edwardson Christmas greeting card, 1935

People line up in front of the old Hope Mission (bottom) to see King George VI and Queen Elizabeth in May 1939.

Line up for Royal visit, 1939

Ken and Hellen Jasper circa 1947

**Volunteers help paint the "new" Hope Mission on
97 Street and 104 Ave., 1960**

Harold Burma with wife Victoria and sister Anne, the Gospel Tone Trio

Hope Mission 1960-1969, 97 St. and 104 Ave

Sunday School, 1969, Lilly Lewis (2 Row Left)

New Home for Hope Mission, 1970

**Edmonton Journal Sept. 12, 1970, Howard Hunt,
(New home article)**

Bryn Skagen, 1972

Norman Relf

Mrs. Relf, 1973

**First Camp at Stony Hill Farm, 1972,
Ray Buttrey Director**

John Scotty McEwan

Girls Camp at Joseph Lake, 1977

Martha Pehl serving food and dispensing hampers

Rev. Ed Enarson talks to one of the many men seeking spiritual help

Ed Enarson Journal March 1, 1980

**Herb Jamieson, Mrs. Hillie Edwardson and
Bob Bogle, groundbreaking Sept. 20, 1982**

**Bob Bogle presents Harry Strom with plaque
Sept. 20, 1982**

**New Hope Mission built beside older Hope Mission
on 106 Avenue, 1983**

Ed and Shirley Enarson

Herb Jamieson honouring Martha Pehl

Board of Directors, 1985

**Bruce Reith serves watermelon at a
Street Barbeque**

**Hope Mission's Annual Street Barbeques
attract hundreds**

**Maynard Cole being honoured by
Chairman Herb Jamieson**

Herb Jamieson and friends

Doug and Janette Green

Happy child at Christmas Banquet

Hope Mission guest

Ramdeo Persaud

Herb Jamieson Centre

Cathy and Alan Pysar lead Chapel service, 1993

**Sylvia Carbert, Administration Women's Program
Manager from 1986 to 1998**

Mark and Linda Turner

**Cory Swayne (back row left) Manager and first
Youth Home Staff, 1998**

Volunteers help serve at Summer Street Barbeque

Kids in Action youth perform at Hope Mission's annual banquet, 2000

Herb and Henrietta Jamieson

**Youth Sports Centre Sod Turning, August 8 2001
Allen Wells (Tegler Foundation) excited kids and
Herb Jamieson**

Sod Turning with Board of Directors for New Hope
Mission Main Building August 5, 2003

Ministry Van, Ed & Trudy Madge

**Johnny Cash at Hope Mission aka
Chaplain Alan Pysar**

Hope Mission Bargain Shoppe

Kids from Kids In Action

**Brent and Arlene Ankrom, Brightwood Ranch,
Camp Director**

141

Rider at Brightwood Ranch Camp

Line up at Hope Mission's main building

Youth Shelter, 2005

Staff appreciation Bruce Reith recognizing 15 year service of Ed Major

Hope Mission's Immigration Hall

Young Leaders of Hope Mission November 2008

Immigration Hall, Oct 2009, Susan McGee,
Executive Director Homeward Trust, Ben
Henderson, City Councillor-Ward 4, Tim Uppal MP
Edmonton-Sherwood Park, Naresh Bhardwaj, MLA
for Edmonton-Ellerslie, Bruce Reith, Executive

Andrew, Stephen, Scott, Bruce & Karen Reith

**Premier Ed Stelmach poses with over 50 Hope
Mission Recovery program graduates, April 2009**

**Premier Ed Stelmach recognizing Hope Mission
Chairman Ron Hystad, 2009**

In Front of Edwardson Place, Delores & Ross
Edwardson, Dagmar (Edwardson) Cunningham,
Rev. Paul Edwardson, 2009

Toward the Goal:
Transition and Growth

I press on toward the goal for the prize of the heavenly call of God in Christ Jesus (Philippians 3:14).

BRUCE REITH

Rwanda in 1980, although not always peaceful, was still relatively unnoticed. It was an unlikely place to find an adventurous young Canadian with a business background. Bruce Reith was in his mid-twenties when he volunteered as a missionary apprentice with the Southern Baptist Convention. It was, as Bruce explained, "something I felt I was supposed to do."

Bruce was born in Calgary but grew up in Edmonton. As a high school student, he volunteered as a page in the Alberta legislature and early on nurtured an interest in things political. After graduating from high school, he went to Red Deer College for one year. Not sure what he wanted to do in life, he set off to travel through Europe in 1974. Returning to Canada, he worked for CP Air in Terrace, British Columbia.

The following year, back in Edmonton, he enrolled at the U of A, he met some people from the Southern

Baptist Student Union. Through the influence of these new friends Bruce began attending Jasper Place Baptist Church.

To know Bruce Reith is to know that he is not given to ecstatic experience. And so, on Christmas Day in 1976, while praying, he knew that an ultimately profound event had happened. As Bruce described it, "It wasn't *like* God's presence filled the room; God's presence *did* fill the room." From this unique and personal experience of being consumed by the unmistakable reality of Christ's love and mercy, Bruce knew that his life would somehow be wrapped up in service to God. It was a calling, and Bruce began wondering and exploring what this calling might be.

Bruce's close ties with the people in his church, especially with his first mentor, Pastor Marvin Thompson, had a significant influence on his Christian journey. Subsequently, Bruce was led to volunteer for a two-year missionary term through the CP (Co-operative Program) Missions of the Southern Baptist Convention.

The city of Kigali was in every respect a world away, and it was a difficult first few months for Bruce. Nevertheless, he acclimatized to mission life in Rwanda. In large part, his acclimation was thanks to missionary Earl Martin, a seminary professor and a leader's leader. Dr. Martin was Bruce's second true mentor, and he became his close friend. What impressed Bruce about Earl Martin was his genuine personal interest in him and his lack of pretension. Bruce recalled, "He didn't treat me like a junior; he treated me like a colleague." Through this close working relationship, Bruce began to throw himself into his mission work.

While in Kigali Bruce developed a heart for the inner city. He was stationed in the heart of the city and every day witnessed the poverty, crime and destitution of many Kigali people. As he served and got to know some of the residents, an aspiration to work in the inner city deepened. Although this desire was still unfocused, Bruce was indelibly marked by the experiences of his two-year mission term.

Flush with a missionary outlook, Bruce landed back in Edmonton in 1982, wondering what God wanted him to do and where he wanted him to go. He had experienced a life-altering assignment in Rwanda, and his work and dedication to missions hadn't gone unnoticed. Earl Martin had encouraged him to think about enrolling in the seminary in Dallas, getting his master's and returning to Rwanda as a career missionary. Bruce went to the States to visit Earl, but later returned, keeping the option in the back of his mind yet not fully convinced this was what he should do.

He reacquainted himself with Jasper Place Baptist Church and continued to attend there. Laurie Lafleur, Hope Mission's chaplain at the time, also attended the church. Laurie and Natalie Lafleur had been invited by Ed Enarson to join the staff and reside in the new facility to give on-the-scene supervision to the programs of Hope Mission. It was through Laurie that Bruce became acquainted with Hope Mission.

He began to volunteer every week at one of the evening services. "I loved to go down to the Mission," he recalled. "I was working as an office manager at a printing company, but I was bored; the Mission was a highlight for me." Not long after, he met Ed Enarson and expressed his general interest in the work of the Mission. When Bruce heard there was an opening on Hope Mission's board of directors, he inquired about the position. In March 1985, chairman Harold Burma invited Bruce to join the board. Towards the end of the year, Ed Enarson, having reached retirement age, resigned. A few months later, on November 23, 1985, Bruce became the executive director.

APPRENTICESHIP

For Bruce, the years following his appointment were times of learning and growing as a director and leader. But a new dimension was also happily added to his life. Through a mutual friend, who also happened to be a friend and supporter of the Mission, Bruce met Karen Little, whom he married in October 1988. (They now have three sons: Scott, Stephen and Andrew.)

Bruce's third mentor was perhaps his most influential. Herb Jamieson has always been recognized as a driving force behind the presence of many Hope Mission volunteers and workers. For Bruce however, Herb's influence, personally and professionally, was profound. Herb was a spiritual advisor, instructive board member, model leader, confidante and friend. Bruce sums up Herb's influence in his life as "powerful."

Over the years, through many unique challenges, Herb's history and experience were invaluable to Bruce. At the same time, he points to the good fortune of always having key people around him that understood what it took to keep ministry alive and breathing.

Ramdeo Persaud was part employee, part volunteer. He lived in the Mission, and in exchange for his room and board he helped paint and maintain the new facility. Emigrating from New Guinea and finally receiving his landed immigrant status, he continued to work faithfully in a host of roles, from maintenance to program manager to volunteer recruitment and coordination.

Ramdeo's joy was his faith in Jesus, and he radiated this joy and influenced everyone he met. His warm demeanour endeared him to many, and his effervescence excited many about the work of Hope Mission. He was a kind of natural advertisement for the work of the Mission. The event that gave him the most delight was when he finally succeeded in bringing his wife and children to Canada to be with him.

There were other key people, such as Mark and Linda Turner, two steady and long-term employees of Hope Mission. Hired by Bruce, they met at Hope Mission and later married. They understand better than most the value of donations and the counting of inventory to the last garbage bag, so as to keep the Mission afloat. Over the past two decades they've served in more capacities than perhaps they care to remember. Call them mission bluebloods, because to this day they provide the Mission with an anchorage through their model of simple, proficient and faithful service.

The Work of
Hope Mission

DAY PAROLE

What began with visiting inmates in federal and provincial institutions became a significant part of Hope Mission's ministry to both men and women. In 1984, Ed Enarson began a halfway house program as part of a men's outreach initiative. When Bruce Reith took over, he worked hard to expand the program as well as to solidify relationships within the justice and solicitor general's department. This had the effect of giving the Mission added stability as well as preparing it for expanded ministries.

The day parole or halfway house program, supported through a contract with the solicitor general, began with just a few men in 1984. Over the life of Hope Mission's association, the Mission took in and saw through the completion of parole of hundreds of men and women.

The Mission's idea of a halfway house was simply to provide some dignified, positive, faith-rooted community structure while the men and women readjusted to life on the outside. Because of the depth of emotional and psychological anguish many parolees have experienced, this was one of the Mission's most difficult ministries. Past chaplain Vernon Grant observed, "Because hardships are so evident, it's critical we stay close to Christ, as we try to provide personal and spiritual support for these men."

There were failures; there were dark complexities around issues of trust. But also, there were many happy endings. And sometimes what looked like failure was a step forward. The following note was sent to the Mission by a woman who had failed to keep her parole. She was back in jail, and her circumstances looked very bleak. She wrote:

> This note is to reassure you that even though things look bad for me now that I'm back in prison and I have lost my daughter, that *the work done at Hope Mission was not in vain.* I often think about the things that were said and taught. I just wanted you to know.

SUDDEN GROWTH: THE HERB JAMIESON CENTRE

In June 1970, the provincial government floated the idea of private operation of the single men's hostel. For some reason, whether there was a lack of interest on behalf of the social care organizations or resistance within the government, the idea died. For Hope Mission's part it only earned a footnote at a board meeting. It wasn't time.

Twenty-two years later the idea not only resurfaced, it was activated. In 1991, Hope Mission, along with a number of other Edmonton social care agencies, made application to run the single men's hostel.

Built in the late fifties under an act of the provincial government, the hostel had always been managed and maintained by government employees. Under the Progressive Conservative administration it was slated for privatization, and Hope Mission was awarded the contract. Although Bruce Reith and the board felt that the Mission had the capability to put together a good staff and run the social care facility well, the awarding of the contract came as a bit of a surprise because Hope Mission, in many circles, had still been regarded essentially as a soup kitchen.

It takes time for perceptions to change, and it began with the faith step taken by Ed Enarson and the board at least a decade earlier. The building and the subsequent debt retirement of a million-dollar facility showed the Mission as a stable and capable organization. The good light that this cast on the Mission no doubt had a convincing effect on the decision-making panel.

But perhaps the greater satisfaction in getting the contract was that the application made no secret that Hope Mission would be running the hostel as a faith-based agency. The proposal stipulated that the Mission would hire chaplains and found all of its activities, from programs to daily routine, on the Christian faith. None of this was played down. From the perspective of today's cautious pluralism, for a government to award a significant public contract to an openly Christian agency was historic. However, the directors and Bruce Reith saw the awarding of the contract as something more than historic. It was recognized as a gift. Herb Jamieson noted, "Unless the Lord builds the Mission, those who build labour in vain."

The addition of the hostel had a sweeping impact on Hope Mission. Before this, the Mission was a single facility operation with a staff of around twelve full- and part-time employees. But overnight Hope Mission expanded exponentially. The staff roster quadrupled, and the number of in-residence clients the Mission served went up tenfold. It was a new and exciting time.

One of the first orders of business was changing the name of the new facility. Through the initiative of Bruce Reith, the board decided to honour Herb Jamieson by naming the hostel after him. By this time, Herb was an honorary board member and the Mission's acknowledged patriarch. The single men's hostel officially became the Hope Mission—Herb Jamieson Centre in recognition of Herb's long-standing and often long-suffering work and dedication. When given an opportunity, Herb would chide the board in his own particularly blithe way, telling them that if they were really sincere about honouring him and naming a building after him, they might have considered using something other than a street hostel maybe more along the lines of, say, the Westin or Hotel MacDonald.

Geographically, Hope Mission was moving back to its roots. The address of the old Mission hall where Rev. Edwardson served for so many years was a mere stone's throw away from the Jamieson Centre. Yet here, more than six decades later, Hope Mission's new staff found that great needs were still present and that those needs were essentially the same.

On June 26th, 1992, Hope Mission threw itself into this new dimension of ministry. Staff soon learned the challenges and rewards of serving and meeting the basic needs of more than 100 men each day.

Additionally, through a partnership with the Boyle McCauley Health Clinic and Capital Health, the Herb Jamison Centre also offers nursing services for residents and people in the inner city. Besides this, the men are also able to see a social services intake worker on site.

By the following year, as part of the accepted operating proposal, the top floor of the Herb Jamieson Centre's west wing was renovated. Hope Mission was now able to move its halfway house program and develop a treatment program by replacing the large dormitories with individual rooms. The men's programs were now moved over to the Jamieson Centre, leaving the newer building for the development of women's services.

Over the years the demand for services has mushroomed. It is common now for the Jamieson Centre to reach its 250-person capacity. Denis Meier, the current manager of the centre, and his staff and volunteers have the task of creating a welcoming space for each guest. They know that the real ministry takes place in all the small gestures of care in serving lunch, in conversation, in washing soiled clothes, in scrubbing the mats and mopping the floors. Often overlooked, these are nevertheless Christ's chosen areas of service, and in these encounters of common humanity, mutual dignity arises and possibilities for change surface.

Hearts and hands restoring dignity through the love of God is the underscored credo of all that goes on at the Herb Jamieson Centre.

Faith-based Programs

Now hope that is seen is not hope. For who hopes for what is seen? (Romans 8:24).

Larry called the senior chaplain out of the blue. He called to express his gratitude to the chaplains and staff for what they had done for him in the few months he was with the Herb Jamieson Centre treatment program. Larry, an aboriginal man, was the second resident to complete the men's treatment program. At the time of the call he was working at a good paying job in northern Alberta. He was happy and still sober after eight years.

Senior Chaplain Alan Pysar, who has been with Hope Mission since 1992, explained, "We see many apparent failures. Men go back to their addictive lifestyles from time to time, but it's a breath of fresh air when God encourages us through a call such as Larry's." Alan added, "Many of the hundreds of men who have finished our program over the years are just like Larry, doing well and growing in their faith and their recovery."

There are some inescapable facts now emerging and

being reported from across North America, comparing faith-based treatment programs with secular treatment programs. In comparison, the completion rate of secular treatment programs fall behind those that are faith-based, and the rate of recidivism and program re-entry are lower for faith-based treatment. Hope Mission's own treatment programs have consistently graduated more than 25 percent of its program residents. This might not seem like a passing grade unless you understand the depth and nature of addictions. Of course symptoms must be treated, but addressing root causes is the way to affect change. Christians in this ministry understand that only a change of heart precipitates true life change. It is in this hope and based on this faith that Hope Mission's treatment programs are crafted and developed.

What makes a Christian-based treatment program Christian is loving contact. It's entering the mystery of Christ's presence in the presence of one another. It's recognizing that there is a larger love that deeply desires freedom for all.

Hope Mission Graduates

Every spring Hope Mission celebrates the lives of those who have come through its recovery programs— programs that are now integral to Edmonton's inner-city community. At this year's eightieth anniversary gala, attended by more than 800 of its supporters including Premier Ed Stelmach, Hope Mission also showcased its history and growth. But the fifty-three men and women who graduated from Hope Mission's Breakout and Wellspring recovery programs were the focus of the evening.

Paul, one of the graduates from Breakout, spoke about his experience of abuse through his childhood, his subsequent life on the street, and finally his arrival at the doors of Hope Mission as a result of a near fatal overdose.

"I was lonely; I was a lost soul with nowhere to go," he said, recounting how Denis Meier, manager of Hope Mission's Herb Jamieson Centre, told him whenever he saw him that he was loved. Paul, his voice breaking, said, "Denis praised me even if I was only sober for a day— and he hugged me, even when I was dirty and smelled bad." Paul has been clean for close to two years and is now employed as an intake worker at Hope Mission.

Tanya lived on the streets for two years, enervated by an addiction to crystal meth. She described a violent and tragic upbringing that preceded her homelessness. Tanya, having graduated from Wellspring, is now in her own apartment, reunited with her daughter and planning a counselling career.

Premier Stelmach acknowledged the "powerful impact" of the work of the Mission, saying, "Tonight I've had the honour of witnessing faith in action." In touching on his government's ten-year plan to end homelessness, the premier recognized the larger dimensions of poverty and homelessness. "While shelters meet an immediate need, they do not change lives."

What *does* change lives, as evidenced by the life stories of each of the graduates, is a community of support, a sensitivity to the needs of both body and soul, and compassionate personal engagement.

During his address, Stelmach said, "It's so easy to see the hand of God at work in the Hope Mission."

BREAKOUT RECOVERY COMMUNITY

It was Monday morning, and Michael's appearance was overdue. Michael, who was in the treatment program, hadn't been seen since the previous evening. Chaplain Alan Pysar went up to his room to check on him. When there was no response to his knocking, he entered using his passkey. Michael was hanging off the side of the bed, supported by a belt, which he had used to tie himself down. Beside him were three empty pill bottles that had contained tranquilizers and antidepressants. He was nearing the end of the convulsions and spasms and obviously dying. An ambulance was called, and he was rushed to the Royal Alexander Hospital, where he was resuscitated.

From his perspective, Michael's attempt to kill himself was the only option left at resolving his past   a past haunted by failed attempts at recovery, a girlfriend who prostituted herself for their cocaine addiction, no hope, and nothing to look forward to.

Michael's life is not an anomaly among the men who enter Hope Mission's treatment program. All are in various degrees of bondage to their past. When the New Testament apostle talked about forgetting what is behind and straining ahead (Philippians 3:13-14), he was talking about a life that is doing its homework and so is always in the process of being healed—always in the process of becoming whole. This is the process of treatment.

But this kind of treatment usually happens slowly in the dawning discovery that God loves with abandon and without condition. The single most effective way for someone like Michael to experience this as a possibility is through those around him—his chaplain, loving volunteers and staff, and other caring residents. When the love of Jesus is modelled, even falteringly, a whisper of hope is heard. This penetrating love can then destroy unhealthy self-reliance, begin to heal and finally compel someone like Michael to face the past with courage and risk himself in God's forgiveness while forgiving others.

After spending a week in the Royal Alexander, Michael returned to the Breakout program. Chaplain Alan reflected, "Swirling through Michael's mind the night of the suicide attempt were thoughts of God's punishment and overbearing expectations. Driven by a mixture of real and false guilt over his girlfriend's prostitution for cocaine, compounded by a distorted view of God, Michael chose to escape the desperation and hopelessness." But Alan pointed out, "It was through his own attempted suicide that God began to reveal to Michael something of his unending love." Michael was not rejected. He was invited back, cared for and loved. He was given a new chance and shown possibilities for a new life through a reoriented heart.

In Michael's own words, "Being in this program has saved my life. You can get well here if you're serious about it. God has given me hope and a will to live again." Michael adds, "There are people who care about me here, and the greatest thing I've learned over the past month in the program is that God loves me! I don't have any more doubts about this."

Alan Pysar said of the program, "It's not for those who need it but for those who *know* they need it and genuinely want it." About Michael, Alan added, "He's a walking miracle who had to face near-death before he could receive a new life transformation. Blisters on Michael's ankles, the size of oranges, caused from the friction during Michael's convulsing, now remind him of the pain endured by Christ for him."

There is a kind of motion and rhythm to treatment. It's like the tacking of a sailboat as it makes its way into the wind. There may be long periods when it appears the destination is slipping behind the horizon, but these turn out to be necessary manoeuvres that finally displace the paralyzing effects of regret and despair. They are movements of faith.

BREAKOUT TO TRANSITIONAL HOUSING TO EMPLOYMENT

Perhaps the most gratifying experience is watching the progress of someone who stumbles through the doors of Hope Mission, enters our recovery community and emerges as an employee of the Mission.

ED VISO: BELGRADE TO EDMONTON

Edin (Ed) Viso's Yugoslavian army unit conducted a raid. A few men were captured and interrogated at gunpoint. One of the prisoners said he recognized Ed. The prisoner, after being roundly threatened, still insisted that he remembered Ed. He asked Ed if he'd been at a specific location two days prior. Yes. He asked if it was Ed who pulled out a Marlboro cigarette and threw the empty pack into the garden. Yes. Then he told Ed he'd seen him through the scope of his sniper rifle—he'd chosen not to shoot Ed that day. Ed said, "I chose to protect him. I've never forgotten him."

This is one memory Ed Viso has kept. Most others he has tried to forget in order, he said, to stay sane.

Ed grew up and was educated within the ethnically diverse Socialist Federal Republic of Yugoslavia. His mother was Serbian and his father Croatian. Ed's education, interests and talent led him to become a successful writer. His popular novels—five in all—were published in Yugoslavia. But the country Ed loved, once held together by the statecraft and sheer will of Josep Tito, disintegrated into ethnic aggression and bloody war less than a decade after Tito's death.

Ed recalls that it was four in the morning and he was drinking coffee when the shelling started. Three hundred Belgradians were killed in two days. The first guy Ed saw had lost his foot. Someone else had his scalp peeled back and his brain was showing. Ed replaced the scalp and bandaged him up. "You see a big pile of human meat, no arms, no legs," said Ed, "justice don't exist...not in war."

The violence and lawlessness all around Ed lent legitimacy to his personal anarchy, and he felt they justified his darker activities. By the mid-1990s, Ed was routinely smuggling cocaine and hash from Istanbul to Belgrade. At the same time, he had begun to drink and use drugs increasingly. In time, his life was fuelled solely by alcohol and cocaine, and the quasi self-sufficient life he had managed to carve out crumbled.

Ed observed, "My self-abuse changed all my thinking. There was no longer any high or escape. So my solution was to escape to a new country."

Ed moved to Toronto, then to Edmonton. From

Edmonton he got work in Yellowknife, Inuvik and Nunavut. "But," said Ed, "my life was still one long air-raid drill—and wherever I went my broken self followed, and from that I couldn't escape."

Two years ago, with nothing left except fifty dollars, Ed limped through the doors of Hope Mission. He saw that the only real choice open to him was to enter the Breakout Recovery Program. Ed soon found himself embarking on much more than a journey of overcoming an alcohol and cocaine addiction. It was a journey of painful self-examination and heartrending reflection.

"It was no quick-fix," stated Ed. "I needed to be patient and persistent—but the beauty of Hope Mission is that here you are given the time you need. My teachers gave me a great gift, the gift of time."

Ed said he takes a cue from the Roman philosopher Seneca, who advised that we count each day as a separate life. Ed asserted, "This present moment is precious...it's the only moment in which I have any power."

His face lit up and his large frame leaned in when relating how, by allowing himself to dwell in these moments and linger in the acceptance and love shown him by Hope Mission staff and his recovery community, things began to shift. He added that as he began to apply his mind to daily prayer, asking for wisdom and guidance, inner change began to germinate and physical health returned.

The air-raid sirens, the strafing and the explosions in Ed's mind have stilled. He has found power in silence and stillness. "Stillness is my stepping stone in connecting with the universal source—God the Father and his Son."

Years ago, while in Germany on route to Canada, Ed cried when he saw a television news clip showing all the old Yugoslavian books being burned. He knew the books he'd written were being burned too. "Now," said Ed, "I think it's a favour. My books were empty pleasure. Thank God that this author touched bottom. And I thank Christ for taking me to Canada and to Hope Mission." Ed is now employed by Hope Mission as an intake worker. As well, he volunteers as a recovery coach and helps lead the Mission's Community Church.

He has also been able to reconnect with his two children. When Ed was in recovery, his sons both living in New York and struggling themselves quit drinking. At the time they had no idea that their father was in recovery. Ed exclaimed, "What is this? Only a direct connection through Jesus!"

Ed has returned to his writing. He has just completed a book about his faith journey and his intimate link with the Mission. He wrote, "Hope Mission is my oasis. It is my island of peace. I no longer need to escape myself. I'm at home in my own skin."

WOMEN'S PROGRAM
WOMEN'S CENTRE: WELLSPRING RECOVERY COMMUNITY

With the move of the men's support programs to the Herb Jamieson Centre, Hope Mission was finally in the position to offer women a residential program. Sylvia Carbert, who had been instrumental to the Mission in various capacities since 1984, took on the project of managing the new women's outreach program. A committee was formed to guide the transition into preparing a women's facility ready to accommodate women with or without children.

After over ten years of male residence and the accompanying male decorative techniques, the timing was right for a major facility facelift. An adopt-a-room program was instituted. Soon, church groups, youth groups and others plunged in. For two months the centre was a blur of scrubbing, painting, stencilling, detailing, more cleaning, and finally furnishings placed with critical finishing touches. The result was that every room would please a discriminating interior decorator's eye.

On November 5, 1994, Mayor Jan Reimer rededicated the building as Hope Mission's Women's Centre.

There is a reason why buildings are called facilities and why Hope Mission's programs are important as long as they "facilitate." When they do—and more often than not, they do—it's a beautiful thing. When energy flows through the systems and structures to people, possibilities flourish and personal encounter is natural. The following is a personal letter that tells of such an encounter through the program at the Women's Centre:

> I am a recovering alcoholic. I came from a dysfunctional family. I had recently left a very abusive relationship. I also have two small children. I lost my children because of alcohol and the abusive behaviour that was in our home.
> I came to Hope Mission in February of this year. When I first came here I came for all the wrong

reasons. I was just coming here to secure myself and my children in another place. I was only thirty days sober. Believe me, I thought I was tough and on the outside I was. Religion, well, I thought nobody's going to push that on me.

On a Tuesday in early April I attended one of Hope Mission's regular evening services downstairs. There was a man there who had been drinking, and he was doing everything he could to interrupt the service, including trying to play the piano. Well you can imagine, here was this woman trying to do the service and he keeps trying to play the piano. Finally the pastor had to sit at the piano and hold the lid down until she was finished. This woman I'm referring to is Joanne [Burkholder], one of the staff at the Women and Family Centre. You see it was with her that I became a Christian.

I had always believed in God, but for reasons of my own, I had put him on the back burner, so to speak. But through Joanne and her beautiful way of showing me God's Word, I asked Christ into my life.

It hasn't been easy though. My sobriety is hard. I have been in the hospital with numerous blood clots on my lungs. There has been one mountain after another. But, what I'm saying is simply this, through all of my trials God has been there, he has walked me through them and guided me in his own wisdom.

Believe me, I still have a long way to go in my recovery. But the staff have been there for me, and I thank them from the bottom of my heart. The group sessions every morning have been good for me, helping me with practical everyday issues of relationships and spirituality. I have also learned a lot from the parenting classes.

I am now five months sober, I have Christ in my life, and I have my children back, who are learning to trust me. Thank you, from a very grateful resident.

Over the past fifteen years there have many of these stories—even as the program has evolved.

The Women's Centre is now located at Edwardson Place. This building, at one time occupied by a religious community of oblates, was given to Hope Mission by the Alberta government in 2005 and renamed in honour of the Edwardsons.

Women's program manager Karen Nelson has deepened the focus of the program to reflect a newer understanding of the process of how women heal. For women who have been traumatized and abused—and who have abused themselves—it's the community that becomes the conduit to health. The name has also been changed to cement this understanding: The women's program is now the Wellspring Recovery Community.

Women's Emergency Centre

On May 1, 2007, Hope Mission's Women's Emergency Shelter opened its doors. The first night twenty-nine women who would have spent the night on the street were offered a mat to sleep on, sandwiches to eat and shower facilities. Hope Mission now provides emergency care to over one hundred women nightly.

The focus of the shelter is not merely to provide basic needs but also to build trusting relationships. The Women's Emergency Centre is a bridge to the Wellspring Recovery Community.

Children and Youth Programs
Kids In Action

In 1994, Rwanda was a killing field. But Bruce Reith's memory of Rwanda was not of carnage. Having served there, the massacre touched him in a personal way. What struck him in particular was the young age of many of the so-called warriors. Young adults and children were caught up in the hate between the Tutsi minority and Hutu raiders.

While Bruce's ministry vision for Hope Mission had long been comprehensive, this event focused and pressed him into actively looking for ways to do more for children. It spurred his desire to begin planning preventative measures. While Edmonton is not Kigali, children are still children and are impressionable. Bruce understood that to impress a child's heart with the love of Christ is to change the course of a life and the course of society.

Rev. Cathy Pysar was given the job of developing the Kids In Action program. As a leader, she saw it as an initiative that would serve to restore lives and prevent many human tragedies.

She and her team set out create a program that would captivate the interest of at-risk kids and open doors for families. The idea was to provide an after-school program for kids in inner-city and low-income areas elementary schools. Games, music, dramas, stories and a hot meal round out a fun and significant time. Kids who might have been left on their own are cared for and are also given a chance to meet Jesus through those who come to care.

The Kids In Action program started in 1994 with one inner-city elementary school. Presently under the leadership of Josh Culling, Hope Mission takes its program to 11 elementary schools, primarily in the inner-city and low-income area of northeast Edmonton. Each week well over 300 children attend KIA.

Josh and his team have also enhanced KIA to offer classroom help and student mentorship. Any school requesting support may have a KIA staff assisting with anything from reading with kids to helping in carrying out a lesson. And mentorship, through spending close personal time, can meet a deeper emotional need of a child. The ministry to kids continues to evolve, but it's worth reflecting on one event that helped kick-start the program.

Sometime before the fall of 1994, a Buddhist monk emigrated via a Canadian sponsorship from Thailand to Edmonton. After his arrival, much of his life consisted of involuntary isolation in the basement of a Buddhist temple. An acquaintance of the monk took it upon himself to alert immigration to the inhumane treatment of the monk. At this point Hope Mission became involved. The monk was furtively taken out of the temple and delivered to the Herb Jamieson Centre. The staff, including the day supervisor, Chris Onslow, took a special interest in the monk's well-being. He was vulnerable and his world his way of life was collapsing. A single room was made available at the Jamieson Centre, and the Buddhist monk was given exclusive use of it, so that he could live with some comfort and according to his beliefs.

In time, Chris and social services found him a suitable family on the east side of the city. The social worker whose caseload he was added to was familiar with the situation and impressed that Hope Mission was so considerate to care for this Buddhist monk. The same social worker happened to be a personal friend of the principal of an elementary school and relayed her observations of the Mission's compassion. This unlikely chain of events not only strengthened Hope Mission's relationship with social services, it also opened the door to Kids In Action's first school on the northeast end of the city. The Mission now serves 11 schools across the city.

Because the program is now close to fifteen years old, there are a number of kids who have grown up with Hope Mission. It is gratifying for the Mission and certainly for the leaders of this area of outreach to see these young people take active roles in aspects of the program. Lasting and life-changing relationships have been the result.

YOUTH BREAK

Youth Break was a natural outgrowth of Kids In Action. It was started through some inquiries and contacts at a northeast end junior high school. As more of a low-key program, its primary purpose was to make casual contacts and build relationships with junior high kids.

A parent wrote, "Youth Break has been a real good influence on my daughter. She has become friends with the leaders and looks forward to going each week." A father wrote, "My son has schizophrenia...in the past when he has tried joining groups he has been alienated or asked to leave...Both my wife and I just wanted to inform you of the positive changes in our son. We are relieved to know that he is having fun and being accepted as one of the kids."

At the heart of Youth Break is the art of mentorship. Staff and interested volunteers began to meet weekly, one-on-one, with any young person who was interested. Staff became completely available to the person they mentored. Past program director Cathy Pysar explained, "By far the program that made the greatest difference and had the greatest impact beyond all the planned events and group outings was the one-on-one mentoring. Children opened up, they came out of their shells, pains were shared and trust was built."

Through the ingredients of time and loving attention, lives were shaped, one at a time. One young man is already planning to be a youth pastor because of his experience. When one girl was asked what she'd learned from her mentor, she said, "I learned that when Marilyn said she would be there for me, she was there!"

BRIGHTWOOD RANCH CAMP

For some people, memories of camp may bring feelings of insecurity and adolescent anxiety. For others, feelings of excitement and longing are dominant. For most of us, memories of summer camp are a curious mixture of all of these and more. Whatever the case, our memories remain vivid because they were experienced at a very impressionable time of life and in a setting of high energy and emotion.

Because of this, camp may well represent a turning point, a life transition or a kind of personal milestone. It may have happened that through a word, song, campfire or hug we were pierced by an undiluted conviction-turned-commitment that has never completely left us. This common experience is why Hope Mission has re-established the exuberant, chaotic and joyful life-moulding event that is summer camp.

Hope Mission's camping program history has been sporadic. During several years in the 1970s, there was a good deal of planning and energy put into building and running a summer camp. But circumstances determined its postponement.

In 1996, through a renewed and growing emphasis on children and youth ministry, the summer camp program was resurrected. Adventure Camp started as two week-long camps on rented property. Today, nine five-day camps with a full slate of games, crafts, outdoor activities and recreation—all take place on the Mission's own fully facilitated 220-acre site known as Brightwood Ranch Camp.

Like so many of Hope Mission's past acquisitions, the beautifully landscaped camp set within an alpine valley was a gift. Even its location—a mere hour west of Edmonton—was perfect. In turning the camp over to Hope Mission, former president of Brightwood Youth Ranch Association Mr. Irvin Reich and his wife, Selma, had passed on what had been to them something of a gift.

The Litners, previous owners of the land, lost their five-year-old daughter when a tractor she was riding on overturned on the hill leading up to the present-day staff houses. After the accident, the Litner family moved to Edmonton, where they met Irvin Reich at a church they had begun attending. At the time, Irwin and Selma were looking for land to set up a youth ranch and fulfill a dream. After the Litners' tragic loss of their young daughter, Mrs. Litner had prayed that their farm would not be remembered as a place of death but as a place where young lives might be restored to new life.

Mrs. Litner's prayer has been answered—perhaps beyond what she had ever imagined. In the summer of 2002, the Mission held its first Brightwood Ranch Camp. Over nine weeks, 625 children and youth attended summer camp. And over these past seven years, the numbers have not decreased. During this time, as reported, hundreds of kids have come to know Jesus.

The camp facilities have constantly been improved. New cabins, a new dining hall—even a CNR caboose has been installed. Tracks were donated and installed by CN Railway, and the caboose was a gift from Alberta Prairie Steam Tours, an organization from Stettler.

Recreation areas like the climbing wall, archery range and zip line are a short walk from the cabins. There is a huge hall with a moveable stage and chapel. Of course there are the horses, the corals and stables and many trails. Soon there will be a two-acre lake.

All this has given the Mission an ability to expand and enhance the camp program. There is also the flexibility to offer off-season services. Groups from

Hope Mission's addictions programs have had weekend outings. Special retreats, such as a single mom's retreat, have been held. But summer camp remains the focus.

Understandably, the amount of planning that goes into running a camp hosting some 700 kids is phenomenal. Having everything come together—food, transportation, equipment, staff, volunteers, special speakers and the special requirements that come with children, such as the weekly pre-camp delousing procedure—is something of an organizational triumph. But for camp director Brent Ankrom and the counsellors and the kitchen staff and the volunteers, it's all worth it.

Past counsellor Helena Vander Veen talked about shared tears that occurred when girls allowed their hurt to surface. "It was like a dam had been broken and they really trusted me."

Recalling one special evening after chapel, former camp director Cathy Pysar said, "About 90 percent of the kids just decided to stay and sing and worship. I'm not quite sure how to describe it, but it was like we were in the presence of God—nobody wanted to leave. There were tears and hugs, and kids were touched by God."

Laura Green, a former long-term key worker with Adventure Camp and supervisor of Kids In Action, wrote about taking groups of kids canoeing. "We would glide through the reeds along the shore, picking lily pads, crouching low under overhanging branches. Then we'd check out the old beaver house and collect smooth sticks that the beaver had prepared for us." What struck Laura about these outings was that children could be children again. She said, "It was during these times that the kids seemed to leave all their worries behind."

Laura recalled that the return trip often turned into a race between all the canoes. "During one race back my group was all smiles because we were in the lead. They were so excited. This lasted for about ten seconds; then we were second. Then they told me that second was actually the best place to be and kept smiling and trying hard. Then another canoe passed us. They then said that third place was really the best place to be and kept up the same effort. We returned to the shore, and they were happy as could be coming in third. I found this very interesting because we only had three canoes on that trip."

Chaplain Alan Pysar had the occasion to be one of the camp speakers. He recalled, "To see most of the kids come to Christ with many weeping in the arms of their counsellors on the last evening was a memorable sight. But the highlight of the week was the campfire singsong we had after the service. To see about sixty kids and staff worshipping with hands raised in uninhibited praise was a sort of 'joy unspeakable,' a once in a lifetime memory that I'll always treasure."

Amanda-Lynn, a young camper, wrote to Hope Mission:

> What I remember most about camp is all the smiles from the counsellors and the campers, everyone at camp seemed to be enjoying themselves constantly. There were of course some "bad" days, I fell off a horse and I did get the smallest bed in the cabin. But then I met one of my new best friends, Shilo.

I learned about God too. I learned that God gave everything he could and did everything he could to help us. In the end he helped us in the best way possible; he died on the cross for us. I feel that we should only return the favour and follow his example. To help anyone in need or just to help, to be kind, and to help others understand about him.

Camp was totally awesome, and they had really cool games. My favourite was when we had to put makeup on the counsellors through nylon because it stayed on their faces and in their hair for at least three days!

Of course there are disappointments. Occasionally, in more extreme behavioural situations, kids have to be sent home. As former camp director Cathy Pysar offered, "It's distressing seeing kids who having been touched by God go home and then have the experience turn into a faded picture because there isn't the support." She was quick to add, "But Jesus still touches their lives."

This touch comes in a shared smile and in a funny spontaneous moment, through a word of encouragement and during a special time or prayer shared by just two. It can even come at a moment of discipline.

Current camp director Brent Ankrom and his wife Arlene believe that "if you touch kids now, you touch them forever." And every year there are hundreds that respond to a loving and accepting touch. "Perhaps," said Brent, "it is because there is so much brokenness in these young lives that God takes special care to touch hearts through ordinary people."

Brent knows this first-hand. Having come through a troubled upbringing, it was a camp experience that changed his life's direction. Brent explained, "Christian camping has been in my blood ever since I was sixteen. I went to camp through an inner city youth organization in Winnipeg when I was nine, accepted Christ at camp when I was fifteen and started as a counsellor the next summer. I was asked that year what I wanted to do with my life, and I said I wanted to be a camp director. Most of the significant decisions and times of growth for me have happened while serving at camp."

Hope Mission's camp program is probably summed up best in the aphorism that Brent and Arlene Ankrom and the staff live by: *Building Lives Worth Living.*

YOUTH HOME

In late 1997, another youth service opportunity presented itself. Alberta Children and Family Social Services approached Hope Mission to inquire about placing children in care. They were in need of homes that would take at-risk youth. Because of a lack of space, they were forced to place youth in motels in the care of one-on-one support workers. The Mission accepted the opportunity, and on March 2, 1998, the Hope Mission Youth Home was officially opened.

Ostensibly, the youth home was a receiving and assessment home. It was a short-term care facility that provided emergency care for youth between twelve and eighteen years of age. The young people who are taken into care and arrive at the home are there for a variety of reasons. None of the reasons are good. They all have to do with relationship breakdowns from neglect, abuse, violence and self-abuse. While at the youth home, these young people have the opportunity to experience some stability and loving structure. Ideally, they will move on to foster care or a more permanent group home or perhaps return to their families.

Cory Swayne, who had worked in Hope Mission's women's ministry for over six years, became the youth home's first manager. Cory's direct and simple aim was to plant seeds. She explained, "If we can help the youth understand that there is hope and that they have the power to affect the course of their lives, then we have been successful." Even though the time that the Mission has with the youth is limited, Cory and her staff desired "that each young person would leave here with a message of hope through an experience of care and compassion."

The youth home's first location was on the third floor of the Women and Family Centre. This was an interim arrangement for six youth until a proper house could be found. As expected, it was difficult to have both the youth home and the women's program operating within the same facility. Finally an acreage and residence in Winterburn were located. Some renovations were done, and the six youth moved in. This, however, was a lease arrangement, and because of the kind of youth Hope Mission cared for and the occasional damage to property, the Mission needed to find and purchase its own home. This happened ten months later.

In the fall of 1999, the Bonnie Doon Youth Home was opened. As a government receiving and assessment facility, the home needed to go through social services certification to retain its contract with the provincial government. The house and its program passed. This was followed by the hiring of Dan and Judy Marchuk, a couple with experience and big hearts for this kind of work. As a result, Hope Mission's youth home experienced greater stability and a greater missionary spirit.

GOSPEL IN ACTION

Tom was mixed up in street gangs. In fact, he had grown up around them. But now Tom was on parole—not too uncommon among some of the youth at the home. Because of a breach of his conditions, Tom was turned in and sent to prison, all the while hoping that someone would bail him out. Bail was set at $1,000, which discouraged other gang members from posting bail. Curiously, the youth home received a call stating that for some reason the ledger read $1,000 when the actual bail was $200. The parole officer who called wondered if this corrected figure might be manageable for anyone who cared to get Tom out before the right figure was published for others to see.

It didn't take Dan Marchuk and support worker Randy Loewen long to decide what to do. Within hours, Tom again found himself in the safety of the Bonnie Doon Youth Home. The next day he approached Dan, who was at the computer. Standing behind Dan, Tom put his arms around the man and buried his head in Dan's shoulder. With tears and stammers, Tom thanked Dan repeatedly. Then he said, "You did something my own dad wouldn't do."

Tom's heart was softened, but he wasn't the only one affected by this chain of events. Other kids in the home who had first voiced their indignation over turning in Tom were now amazed that the very people who would do this were also the first to come to his assistance. For everyone, including Tom, this was an act of justice, quickly followed by grace and mercy. This was the gospel in action.

The youth home ran for close to five years. Its resources and energy later shifted to the youth outreach centre. While in operation, it was a place where many people like Tom came into contact with a message of hope and an experience of love.

R.W. Tegler Youth Sports Centre

The vision for a youth outreach centre had been on the mind of Bruce Reith for years. In the late nineties, dreaming, speculation and some preliminary detective work paid dividends and made the centre a serious possibility.

Location of the facility was obviously an essential consideration. Since 1995, Hope Mission has been active in child and youth ministry in the low-income multi-ethnic areas of northeast Edmonton. So when a block of land went up for sale in that area, legal inquiries were made. Everything, including soil tests and surveys, came back in a positive light. With the extensive help of lawyer and mission chairman Jim Odishaw, Hope Mission struck a deal with landowner, Shell Oil. The title was transferred to Hope Mission in December 2000. And on July 8, 2001, the Mission held a groundbreaking ceremony for its new youth centre.

Even before this, the need for an initial funding partner had to be met. The project was going to cost over a million dollars. Not since the building of the Mission in 1982 had the board taken on a project of this scope. The Mission's long relationship with the Tegler family once again proved fruitful, and through the Tegler Trust, the Mission received the seed money and a financial commitment with which to begin the project. Because of the continuous support of the Teglers, the new centre was completed in 2002 and named The R.W. Tegler Youth Sports Centre.

The evolution of Hope Mission's ministry to young people made the youth sports centre possible. Contact with the children and the parents of this community over the past six years through Kids In Action and Youth Break had set the foundation for this endeavour.

The idea of an evangelical outreach youth centre with a sports emphasis is not original to Hope Mission. Bruce Reith and past manager Allen Rempel made contact with The Edge in Winnipeg and Skate Church in Portland and benefited from their insights and experience.

The year-round youth sports centre has a 7,200 square foot vaulted space for skateboarding, in-line skating, BMX biking and wall climbing. Besides a games and lounge area, there are also classrooms for mentorship programs, tutoring, and teaching computer skills. The Centre has space for up to ninety kids at a time. Fifty youth have the opportunity to skate and wall climb while another forty can participate in games and other activities.

Sports such as skateboarding and activities like hip-hop and rap are a natural bridge to capture the attention and enthusiasm of today's kids. The popularity of these sports is still growing, and in a northern climate the substantial bonus of having these activities indoors is obvious.

The kids are in the care of enthusiastic, empathetic and truly supportive Christian staff and volunteers. With the evolution and addition of programs like clubhouse, rhythm, and creative media, the youth sports centre has become a natural place for forming relationships with kids in the community and has given them an alternative to crime and gang-related lifestyles. The youth sports centre has helped reduce crime, drug abuse and vandalism, and it has supported families and built up the community.

A Word About HYMN

HYMN, the *Hope Mission Youth Ministry Network,* is a collaborative initiative of Hope Mission's youth ministries—Brightwood Ranch, R.W. Tegler and Kids in Action. While each ministry offers its own unique services and programs, what they have in common is the desire "to sow positive seeds into the lives of the youth of this city." Collectively, they are Hope Mission's preventative ministries, and it made sense for them to work together more closely. Hence, HYMN was born.

The vision doesn't stop with Hope Mission. The intention is to network the city. Ideas and possibilities, ministry opportunities, success stories and news of the events put on by like-minded organizations and individuals can be accessed through a common link, www.wearehymn.com. HYMN hopes to develop and keep the communication lines of city-wide youth ministry open, accessible and exciting. If it's happening, HYMN has it covered.

Youth Shelter

"Thank you for giving me and every young person who comes to the shelter a second chance." This is the way Ryan C. ended his address to over 800 supporters at Hope Mission's eightieth anniversary banquet in April 2009. It was a heartfelt and moving thank you, as well as a plea to not give up caring about the youth in Edmonton.

Two years earlier, controlled by booze and pills and often sleeping where he dropped, Ryan found and connected with the youth shelter. But after a brief time he was back on the streets—and this time things got even more serious. When he was released from jail, he went back to the shelter and was determined to apply himself to the program.

The youth shelter began in a double-wide trailer in the parking lot of the Herb Jamieson Centre in 2004. In 2008, the newly renovated second and third floors of the original 1980 Mission became the permanent home of the youth shelter. The shelter accommodates up sixty boys and twenty girls on an emergency basis, with twelve single-bed rooms for young people in "Shift" a long-term care and support program.

Each of the forty to eighty young people who come to the shelter each evening bring their own unique wounds, wounds that may have been self-inflicted or inflicted through neglect, abuse or exploitation. Often it's a complexity of these things. Resentment, anger, violence and defensiveness become ways of survival, complicated, almost as a matter of course, by drug abuse. Added to the hurt is almost always a disrupted education. The result is a fenced-off life, resistance to care and suspicion of guidance. The barriers of fear and mistrust suffused with shame, a broken self-image and often self-loathing ultimately become barriers to hope and faith.

That is why manager Ryan Harding says his goal is to "continue to try and break down those walls that so many youth have." Ryan and his staff try to engage every person. Not everyone is receptive, but all are welcomed. And for anyone approaching a desire to change, in-depth help is perennially available.

At the right time, Ryan C. was ready to receive this help. He hasn't often looked back. Family relationships have been restored. Despair has given way to faith. A void has been filled by purpose and promise.

A NOTABLE EXPANSION

The significant increase of men and women seeking emergency shelter required a much larger building. The Mission had already installed bunk beds in the Herb Jamieson Centre dorms, and the lower floor of the Women's Centre was used for overflow. But this was a temporary fix. What it didn't do was help address the deeper causes of the growing problem of homelessness.

In October 2004, Hope Mission held its grand opening for the Hope Mission Centre, the Mission's most ambitious expansion to date, made possible by a grant from Homeward Trust. Built to encompass the Women's Centre and taking up all the available real estate, including the area where the old Third Christian Reform Church once stood—was a new three-storey, 65,000 square foot facility.

What's unique about the centre is its "continuum of care" concept. The facility has four phases of residency. The basement floor provides an intox-detox centre for up to seventy occupants. On the main floor, emergency accommodation utilizing mats is offered. On the second floor, forty rooms are set aside for transitional housing, with treatment and support programs. The third floor consists of twenty-four bachelor suites that offer transitional housing or long-term supportive living.

The Hope Mission Centre gives the Mission the opportunity to offer enhanced care and support. People who have become accustomed to living on the street now have an opportunity to access safe, supportive and affordable housing. It has allowed for the creative care for thousands of people, and the housing phases have helped hundreds of men gain the skills, training and counselling needed to enable them to transition successfully into the community and into long-term supportive housing or market housing.

MINISTRY VAN

"The people who run the Hope Mission van are modest about the life-changing work they do, but there is nothing modest about the life they saved tonight." So began Shaw TV reporter Tracy Tripp's coverage of the rescue of a man who accidentally burned his tent down.

It was deep winter with temperatures dipping down to 25 below when the Hope Mission Ministry van responded to a call in the river valley. A candle had tipped over inside a tent, and there was a fire. By the time the ministry van got there the fire had spread, endangering the life of the man who was asleep inside the nylon shelter.

A short scramble through bush took the staff to the burning tent, where the man inside was awakened and helped to safety. Confused and in partial shock, he was safely in the shelter before he recognized how close he'd come to being severely burned or asphyxiated.

Other than the large Hope Mission logo, the ministry van looks like every other ambulance in the city, although it doesn't have all the flashing alarm lights or the loud siren. Then again, the ministry van isn't there to provide medical care; it's there to provide personal and practical care to people in crisis on the street.

It all started as a pilot project in partnership with the Emergency Response Department and the Edmonton Police Service. It was Constable Ashley Emerson of the Edmonton Police Service who suggested the idea while completing a problem-solving project as part of his recruit training. He explains, "I worked in the downtown division and spent a lot of time picking up people who were intoxicated and referring them to social agencies. I spoke with emergency response personnel and realized they dealt with the same thing." So Constable Emerson looked at how similar mobile units were being used in Winnipeg and Vancouver and brought the idea to Edmonton. "I knew this project would be a great option for everyone. Not only does it relieve pressure on emergency personnel, it also gets proper help to individuals who need it. We were ultimately looking to be more efficient and utilize our resources. We want to police to work smarter not harder."

As far as the Mission is concerned, executive director

Bruce Reith noted, "This project fits exactly with what Hope Mission does. We are helping those in special need and at the same time freeing up ambulances to deal with emergencies. The coordinated effort helps us get people off the street and into a place where they are safe, warm and cared for."

While on a ride-along, former Edmonton mayor Bill Smith saw first-hand what the ministry van can provide. "I am very impressed and excited by this van. It's a tremendous service…it provides relief for police and paramedics while ensuring people with afflictions are being taken care of properly and safely."

The ministry van has become an indispensible part of inner-city care. This is especially true during the winter months when the cold threatens the lives of people stranded on the street. Overall, it has become an integral part of Hope Mission's ministry.

HOPE MISSION COMMUNITY CHURCH

The official kick-off of Hope Mission Community Church was on the first Sunday of January 2007. It coincided with the Mission's first annual memorial service for deceased friends of Hope Mission and drew the buzzing attention of three major television networks.

The church had a far more humbling beginning, which had started as a question: If the Mission is "the church in action," why shouldn't it encompass a worshipping church for those it served? This was the simmering query that kept presenting itself to senior pastor Alan Pysar and Bruce Reith, among others.

So it made sense to begin the church as a kind of supportive community for the men in the program. For those in recovery, street survivors who desire a church community, it's not an easy thing to enter the doors of a suburban church. And it's not always easy for a church beyond the inner city to accommodate someone who is slowly piecing his life together—a life once rife with abuse of various forms. It was this understanding and concern that drove the vision and eventually birthed the church.

What started as a loose gathering of a couple of dozen men is now, two and a half years later, a vibrant church of seventy to eighty attendees, a third of which are women. The church has also spawned Soul Sisters, a women's support ministry that meets monthly. A solid team of staff and volunteers—many who have come through the Mission's programs—lead the church in a great variety of musical flavours, from Alan Pysar's incarnation of Johnny Cash, to rock, blues and bluegrass, as well as drama, Bible readings and even preaching.

HMCC leaders like associate pastor Norman Weatherly, Mel and Marybelle Cruikshank, and senior pastor Alan Pysar count themselves privileged to have been a small part of people's lives at HMCC. Alan explained,

> Peter Pham, one of HMCC's leaders, who three years ago was a Breakout Program resident. He was suicidal as a result of a chronic gambling addiction. Now he's a supervisor at the Herb Jamieson Centre, responsible for the guys on the medical wing, and for the Centre's evening services. He now preaches and leads with me and

others in evangelism and music at the Mission's evening services. He loves the Lord and just as important loves the people he serves. He cares for them with a passion that only comes from the hope that Hope Mission has given him.

Lyle Richer has a similar story. He now has over three years of recovery and works on intake at the HJC. He's also a primary worship leader in the church. He recently preached his first sermon at an evening service, and had his first altar call with three-quarters of the 50 or so residents responding for prayer and commitment to the Lord. All of the leaders of IIMCC have similar stories. I'm so blessed to see the growth in them over these few short years.

HOPE BARGAIN SHOPPE

Generous people make it possible for Hope Mission to supply people in need with clothes, shoes, blankets and a host of other necessary items. It has been this way from the beginning when the Mission took up the challenge of delivering care packages to rural areas in the "hungry thirties."

Today the Mission is still blessed by generous donations, so much so that the donation of a warehouse was both timely and critical.

Of what the Mission receives, it gives away all that it can. Everything that is useful is given to clients free of charge. Things such as hygiene items and clean, warm clothing help meet their physical needs and give them a greater sense of dignity. Hope Mission also helps other agencies that work with the poor or new immigrants, in an effort to recycle and use everything possible.

However, not everything received can be given away, and so the Mission took the practical step of opening a bargain shop. What can't be used by guests or given away to good benefit is put up for sale, with the proceeds going back into Hope Mission.

FOOD SERVICES

Sharing good food is at the visceral centre of Hope Mission and yet it's something that occasionally gets overlooked as a ministry. The fact that the Mission now serves over 34,000 meals per month, as well as catering and hosting seasonal banquets and barbecues for hungry men, women, youth and children, should encourage people to never take the Mission for granted.

Feeding the poor is the most tangible of all ministries. Perhaps because of its practicality, it is also the most effective ministry. The sharing of a meal is understood universally, and at Hope Mission it's the first contact, the first experience of care, a guest will have. That first impression is a potential gateway to a new direction and a lasting relationship.

"It's the doorway to the rest of Hope Mission," said Lindy Dowhaniuk, the food services and special events manager. "We try to create an environment—in the way we prepare and serve food—that someone receiving a meal would sense they are valued. We receive people with love...and we believe those who come to us all deserve unconditional respect."

Lindy's philosophy is about valuing human relationships over structural ones. So while the food services team is dedicated to being good stewards of the resources entrusted to them by supporters, they also strive to make sure the nutritional and health needs of those struggling with daily life are met and even exceeded.

Lindy explained, "We're totally committed to dignity. So we treat one another with consideration, and we show compassion to all who come to us. As a ministry of basic and essential care, our hope is simply to open up the possibility for healing, redemption and change. We do this by serving with love."

Rapid Exit

For a homeless person, the term *rapid exit* means going from the street to having a home while essentially bypassing an extended stay in a shelter. It's a fast track out of a shelter and into an apartment.

The theory is simple enough. Give a home to people who don't have homes. Then support them toward a healthy degree of independence to where they can pay rent, work on problem areas in their lives and generally grow in life and relationships by connecting to a community. As Rapid Exit coordinator Ryan McCormick explained, "It's a strategy that has been put to use effectively in several cities across North America and has been proven to both reduce homelessness and save money."

Ryan understands both the theory and the practice. His team, over the first six months of the program, have placed over 120 people into their own homes.

This big thing that we're able to provide that many other social and government agencies don't or can't is relationship. Without a relationship of trust and respect we're seen as just another handout—unconcerned and unconnected with the people we serve. Relationship is at the heart of what we do.

Sometimes this relationship plays out in interesting ways. For instance, one night I was taking out the recycling from my house and in the alley I ran into a guy that I knew from my time working in the shelter. I hadn't seen him in at least a year, and he told me that it was because he had left town but was now back because he needed surgery on his finger. He was living just out behind my house, and he showed me the little camp he had patched together from things he had found in dumpsters. He's an older gentleman and a remarkably sweet guy. We ended up talking for quite a while, and I told him at the end about what I was doing and that if he decided that he wanted a place, to come and talk to us.

It was a few weeks later when I saw him at my office door. I welcomed him in, and we did an "intake" with him. Within a couple of weeks, he was in his own place with his own keys. It's amazing to see the change in him now that he has a place of his own. He stops in often, usually on his way to get some errands done. He's always off to some appointment, whether it's getting his I.D. back, opening a bank account, or getting fitted for new dentures (imagine being on the street with no teeth!). He's even gained some weight and looks healthier each time I see him. He loves having things to do that aren't just about survival. He feels purposeful. It's an amazing feeling to have him sit in the office or to visit him in his own home and talk about anything from little day to day things to big life goals and dreams. I'm thankful that through this we get to be agents of God's grace to people. I'm thankful that by God's grace, a chance encounter in an alleyway led to a man now having a home and a new lease on life.

VOLUNTEERING AND BEYOND
DOUG GREEN

Doug Green's association with Hope Mission began in 1974. He started by leading an evening service every month on behalf of his church, Bethel Gospel Chapel. His skill in passionately communicating the gospel was soon apparent, but what set Doug apart was his love for Christ and compassion for people.

Doug came to Canada during World War II and trained as a pilot in Calgary under the Empire Training Scheme. During this time, Doug recalled, "God spoke very definitely to me through the preaching of the gospel—but also through an air crash involving two of my fellow Australians. It was this that challenged me to fully surrender my life to Christ."

While attending church in Calgary, Doug met Janette, and they were engaged. After the war was over, Janette went to Australia with other war brides and fiancées on a troopship. Janette and Doug were married in November 1945. In 1951, they returned to Canada to care for Janette's aging parents.

Doug got a job with Imperial Oil and worked for the company for thirty-one years. He took advantage of an early retirement package because, as Doug put it, "I just felt I wanted to serve the Lord more fully in my remaining years." So at sixty years of age, Doug went back to school, and while volunteering as a counsellor at Hope Mission, he obtained a master's of theological studies. In 1988, he resigned his position as a board member, where he had already served for several years, and became a full-time staff member.

Doug threw himself into Mission work. He loved it. He was never happier than when he could visit and counsel inmates in prison or when they came to the Mission on day parole. He had time for everyone, and guys from the street would line up to talk to him. His desk was often littered with scraps of paper that diagrammed the salvation story. And the men would listen because they knew they were cared for and accepted whatever their state, whatever their station.

Doug still carries within him the spirit and the intent of Hope Mission. Before his retirement he was a mentor and a model; for those on the streets or in prison, he was an inspiration and a friend. He is a man of prayer with an evangelist's heart. Anyone who knows him knows he prays "at the drop of a hat." Given half a chance—and Doug had a beautifully natural way of creating those half chances—he will tell you about what Christ means to him and what he can mean to others. In a most unassuming and loving way, he will ask people if he can pray for them. Very few refuse.

Doug is generous to a fault. Often he would give away any money he happened to be carrying. The receptionist, feeling some concern for his wife, Janette, would often ask for Doug's wallet when he arrived at work. And occasionally, sensing the wisdom in this, he would check it in. Many in the inner city are indebted to him, but Doug sees this in a different light. He believes he is indebted to them, because through them he was able to serve his God.

Driven by a single and uncomplicated purpose to express and be an expression of the love of Jesus Christ, Doug epitomizes what Hope Mission desires to be. About his retirement from full-time Mission work in the spring of 1998, he wrote, "It has been a joy to work at the Mission. And I believe it was the place God wanted me to serve. My desire has been to lead people here to accept Christ as Saviour, and, through practical care and concern, for them to see Christ living in me." This desire of his was granted.

MAYNARD COLE

Eva and Hans Rasmussen, from the Calvary Lutheran Church, volunteered with Hope Mission's Sunday school for several years during the sixties. At the time there were a large number of Métis and other aboriginal children who attended. This ministry to aboriginal children and parents eventually led the Rasmussens to the Saddle Lake Reserve.

Maynard Cole attended the same church as the Rasmussens, and it was their influence that sparked Maynard's interest in Hope Mission's outreach. Eva had been able to meet the parents of two siblings who came to the classes. Through the relationship that she built, and through her care for their children, both the mother and father became Christians. Maynard's first assignment with Hope Mission was to keep the connection open and, through a weekly Bible study, lead the parents in Christian growth.

Maynard recalled they were very receptive, but "the father still had an alcohol problem, and they moved away to a place on the south side. But I found them shortly, and I kept on visiting them."

Over the years Maynard's patience and loving persistence showed in many other ways. He taught Sunday school and helped clean and maintain the Mission, all out of a conviction to be of use to God. Very little kept Maynard from what he saw as his duty to serve. In November 1977, he helped tear down the old parsonage where Hope Mission's Youth Centre now stands. Just before the completion of the project, a stepladder he was standing on collapsed, and he fell, fracturing his ankle. Maynard noted, "Eleven days later I was back at work down there."

Maynard's work changed in the late seventies and eighties. He began helping with the venerable Mission practice of picking up food donations from various grocers and doughnut shops. After this, he would help sort the edible from the inedible for serving at the evening services. Then he would fill food hampers that would be given to inner-city residents. Martha Pehl, another irreplaceable volunteer, took charge of the final sorting. Maynard said of Martha, "She was a very kind-hearted woman, but sometimes she had harsh words when I failed her in some way, and she had me crying once."

He recollected that Ramona Klymok, with the help

of her husband, Richard, took over Martha's job, as she was already quite old. Maynard reminisced, "Ramona was a real pleasure to work for...Richard was killed in a car crash a number of years ago, and his funeral was held in Hope Mission, where mine has been arranged by my dear brother in Christ Bruce Reith."

Maynard volunteers from the bottom of his heart and serves "out of the joy of the Lord." To Maynard nothing is menial; all work is ministry. Up until nine years ago, while in his 82nd year, Maynard could still be found riding in the panel truck every Thursday and helping with the donation pickups. When this was done, he would take a garbage bag and pick up all the litter from around the Hope Mission building.

When Maynard talks about his long-term work at the Mission, his face wrinkles up in a smile. "The men that have supervised this place have been wonderful men, kind men." As staff member Eddi Tocaur expressed, "You can just tell Maynard is close to God's heart."

Yuri Novakov

The Mission is very thankful for all its volunteers, like Yuri, who came to the Mission in 1992 from Belorussia and gave so much of his time, doing everything from housecleaning to security to leading services. After becoming an employee, and while working close to full-time and also battling a chronic degenerative illness, Yuri gained a PhD in linguistics at the University of Alberta. Through all this he managed to bring his mother to Canada. In 2001, he was offered a job in Ottawa as a Russian interpreter. At his farewell Yuri attributed his accomplishments in the face of small and great struggles to "working it out in prayer" and having at hand "encouraging and wonderful people on staff." On surveying his decade of serving at Hope Mission, Yuri said, "My spiritual growth happened here."

For Hope Mission's part, it will flourish by serving as long as God calls to it people with hearts and souls like Doug Green, Maynard Cole and Yuri Novakov.

About Hope Mission's Growth

Credibility cannot be purchased; it is built over time. Hope Mission's startling growth over the past two decades was not sudden. It was made possible through dedicated obedience. Like the bamboo shoot that is watered over many long years and then in one year grows to a great height, so it was with Hope Mission. The recent outward growth of Hope Mission and the ability and poise to be able to meet the burgeoning need were achieved by the watering of continual prayer and by faithful labour over many years.

In 2000, The board of directors modified Hope Mission's mission statement to read "To serve, strengthen and uplift men, women, youth and children through the life-changing gospel of Jesus Christ." This clearly lines up with what Bruce Reith envisioned for Hope Mission not long after his arrival. This vision to serve and to impact the lives of all impoverished people in Edmonton was formed through his Kigali experiences, his mentors' influence and his obedience to a calling. In talking about the Mission's evolution and future, Bruce stated, "We will simply keep relying on God's leading." This reliance has been the way of Mission leaders throughout Hope's history.

Bruce has eclipsed founder Rev. Harold Edwardson's length of service and is now the Mission's longest serving director.

A Good Work—
A Promised Future

I am confident of this, that the one who began a good work among you will bring it to completion by the day of Jesus Christ (Philippians 1:6).

Immigration Hall

After one year of ministry, with barely enough time to get their feet wet, the Edwardsons were plunged into the kind of emergency effort that even with today's equipment and resources would be daunting. They accepted an appeal by the City of Edmonton to daily prepare enough soup or porridge to help give relief to hundreds, even thousands, of unemployed people for the duration of one year. It was a task almost beyond the Edwardsons, but they shouldered the responsibility with conscientious determination.

For this purpose, the old Immigration Hall, which stood a block up the street from Hope Mission, was pressed into service. Built in the mid 1890s, the wood framed two-and-a-half-storey building had been allowing seventy immigrants at a time to gather and begin the adventure of settling into their new home.

Because the original hall had already shown that it couldn't handle the waves of immigrants during the early 1900s, construction of a new Immigration Hall one block east of the old one began in 1930. It was completed in 1931. In 1954, in the middle of another great influx of immigrants, the addition of a wing effectively doubled the space of the hall.

For too many years the Immigration Hall languished in neglect and disrepair and was in danger of being torn down. However, Hope Mission had been keeping its eye on the fate of the hall since its vacancy in the early 1990s because of its proximity, potential for ministry expansion and unique historical connection.

As a result of a long pursuit and tenacious legwork by Bruce Reith and the board, and with the subsequent involvement and vital support of Homeward Trust, Hope Mission finds itself today in possession of the interwar Immigration Hall. With renovations complete, the historical hall contains twenty-three one-bedroom units, plus twenty-one bachelor suites, and is now meeting the needs of former homeless men and women as they move from recovery to independent living. Complementing Hope Mission's continuum of care model, the transitional and long-term supportive housing facility will serve Edmonton's at-risk population for years to come.

The historical significance of Immigration Hall has been preserved. In the first place the redevelopment has stayed true to the classical simplicity and symmetry of early twentieth century architecture. But more significantly—not unlike Immigration Hall's original intent—the practical application of welcoming, accommodating and caring for people who are opening a new chapter in life is preserved. The hall continues to be a gateway through which men and women enter a new life in community.

FULL CIRCLE: PROMISED FUTURE

Todd Maclean, manager of Hope Mission Centre, intercepted a familiar face. It was Carl, rushing in through the front door. Breathless, he asked Todd to call 911, as he had just awakened at the back of the main building and had been unable to rouse his wife, June, at his side. Todd recounted, "When I ran out to check on June, her grey complexion told me all I needed to know; June had passed away. None of Carl's gentle urgings were going to bring her back."

"It's a tragedy," Todd said, "that will stay with me...people who have so little losing what little they have: each other." It didn't make the tragedy less real or less painful, but perhaps for Carl, Todd's presence made it more bearable.

Mission workers work to understand, address and erase the cause-complex of poverty. But Christ's words *"For you always have the poor with you"* (Matthew 26:11) inject a certain reality into this dream. This doesn't mean that the dream is given up. What it does is warn against trusting utopian visions and universal projects. It reminds the Mission of the task at hand—meeting the needs of one person at a time, like caring for Carl in his immediate need and working toward preventing more tragedies like June's, while always pointing to a greater hope deeper within. Staff and volunteers will tell you that when hope comes, when a glimmer seeps into the dark corners, the reward is simply being around to see it.

Still, in working at the Mission there is a sense in which you never get to complete anything—broken hearts and lives have, so far, continued to surface. It's easy enough to see that offering hospitality, entering into the tangle of relationship and creating a sense of community does not admit completion in the way a building project does. In this sense the Mission is always "on the way."

Just as Paul, the apostle, was able to say that he had finished the race and completed the work (2 Timothy 4:7), even though only a few scattered but committed communities of Christ followers were present, Hope Mission is able to say that God has indeed *completed* Hope Mission, because it is alive and present among those Christ came to serve.

The acquisition of Immigration Hall is emblematic of Hope Mission coming full circle, as well as its hopeful future. The countless lives that have been touched and the lives yet to be touched testify to a kind of dynamism of having already run the race in the face of a horizon of "not yet."

Over these eighty years many ministry chapters have opened and closed. Yet on a profound level, Hope Mission has always been a harbour of hope for people in need.

A Legacy of
"Church in Action"

Religion that is pure and undefiled before God, the Father, is this: to care for orphans and widows in their distress, and to keep oneself unstained by the world (James 1:27).

Hope Mission's beginning was through the vision of a pastor and his wife. Rev. and Mrs. Edwardson found themselves compelled, through a kind of restless faith, to express their love of Christ through social compassion. In essence they resigned one pastorate for another. Their hearts were wrapped up in the understanding that true religion was about sharing life with the vulnerable of this world. Within the Church, they found the support and strength of like-minded Christians to begin the ministry of feeding the hard-pressed unemployed people of the Great Depression.

Many chaplains, managers and support workers come to the Mission through the Church. Like the Edwardsons they took seriously the words of Christ in Matthew 25:31-46, which tell us that serving the forgotten is serving Jesus Christ.

Hope Mission has had an eighty-year-long history

with the Church, but the history of the relationship between the local Church and the Mission is not a simple or static thing. Because the first board of directors of Hope Mission constituted that the Mission be inter-denominational, which was ratified by subsequent boards, its relationship to the Church has sometimes been seen as less intentional. The Mission, in wanting a broader Church appeal and an ecumenical appeal, took a more difficult path. Perhaps missions that are supported through one denomination have a stability and a sense of ownership that Hope Mission has not been able to have. Yet the Mission has always desired to be embraced by the Church, and it quickly acknowledges that its very existence is deeply rooted in the Church.

Hope Mission is known as a para-church ministry. The best way to understand this is to see the Mission as an arm, specifically a social care arm, of the Church. Unfortunately, *para-church* has sometimes been understood as outside or exclusive of the Church, and so Hope Mission has occasionally been seen as a social agency that happens to be Christian. A better understanding of this relationship is that it is symbiotic. The Mission and the Church live together to the benefit of each other. In this sense the health of Hope Mission is tied to the kind of relationship it has with the Church, and by virtue of this, it is tied to the health of the Church. This also is as it should be.

For Hope Mission's part, it desires to see and encourage evangelical churches to progressively move toward front-line social care in their immediate community. Hope Mission believes it can also be an assistant to the Church's efforts in social care. Those who love the Church want to see it always unfolding and stretching beyond itself not simply enduring, but more often prevailing, as is the hope of Scripture.

The practicality of this relationship is in its mutual support. Over the years a portion of Hope Mission's material support has come through the Church. As well, it is through the Church that much of the Mission's volunteer help comes, and it is through the prayers of the Church that the mission, ministry and spiritual integrity of Hope Mission is upheld. On the Mission's side, the Church can gain the knowledge that could better equip it to serve its local social concerns. Hope Mission is a place of referral that churches feel confident about. Hope Mission can also be a social conscience for the Church.

It is a struggle to move the social teaching of Scripture and the Church into the hearts of people. But this struggle and this incongruity between faith and practice can be overcome. Many people who have come into the inner city and have taken just a fifteen-minute tour find within themselves a stirring or a rekindling of empathy toward the poor. Just as Rev. Edwardson's heart was moved to act as he stood at the construction site of the Leland Hotel and saw the hungry, the desperate and the forgotten turned away because there was no work, those who come in person often hear anew Christ's words *"Just as you did it to one of the least of these who are members of my family, you did it to me"* (Matthew 25:40).

Hope Mission believes that as the Church moves into the future with practical acts of love and relentless social compassion, it will once again find a voice. In obedience to Christ a renewed focus on feeding and caring for the poor has the effect of diminishing the things that divide churches. Out of mutual love for Christ, the Church will find itself moving toward being one in love. Here the Church will not only have a voice because of its social action; it will also have a transforming voice because it is becoming one in love.

A Legacy of Outreach

"Open your hand to the poor and needy neighbor in your land" (Deuteronomy 15:11).

Hope Mission's practice of opening its hands to the poor and needy neighbour is its identity. It was founded by Christians who deeply desired to reach society's marginalized people, those who live in the shadows of the towers of commerce. Here life is shorter, more tenuous, more violent, certainly poorer and, on the whole, much riskier than life in suburbia. But this opening of hands is not without its own peculiar risks, setbacks and disappointments. Light in these inner-city shadows often comes slowly, even imperceptibly.

Success in urban ministry is not evidenced by throngs of inner-city residents with changed lives or crowds who have successfully escaped the trappings of addiction. Certainly there are changed and freed lives, but Mission workers are sometimes profoundly disturbed by the apparent absence of a more wholesale transformation. They may even feel deserted and question the seeming futility of it all, until they are compelled to look deeper. It is then that they learn once again that in the desperation and in some sense *because* of the depth of desperation in these shadows, hope abides. Here, close observation reveals the stubborn presence of promise and possibility in spite of the darkness and the apparent changelessness; this attests to the reality that *light* has indeed come into the world.

But it takes eyes of faith and hearts of hope to see this reality. Over the decades, people with these kinds of eyes and hearts have abandoned themselves to the ministry of Hope Mission. Love, faith, humility and patience are preconditions for discoveries of hope in the darker shadows. They are the job qualifications for mission work.

Growing Hope

I have fought the good fight, I have finished the race,
I have kept the faith (2 Timothy 4:7).

In the midst of societal despair, a few Christians who understood that their hope was not founded on things seen sacrificed their own security and began a ministry of hope. They understood that what protein is to the body, hope is to the soul. So they chose the Mission's name in that light. Through eighty years of service, the name *Hope Mission* continues to act as a succinct ministry statement.

Hope Mission was built in obedience to a call and on a foundation of faith; these twin pillars guide its present and, with God's grace, will govern its future. This faith foundation was evident during a difficult time shortly after the Mission opened. In an interview with LaVyne Osbak, Mrs. Edwardson described one night in the early spring of 1930. Her husband, in anguish, and despairing of any future the Mission might have, spent the night pacing the floor and praying. He repeatedly called out, "Lord, you've opened the door. Lord, you've opened the door..."

Silently an answer came. "I have opened the door, and no man can shut it."

That spring morning as the sun came up and light flooded their little bedroom, Harold told his wife, "We simply can't close the door. We'll just keep going!"

Weeks before her passing in 1983, Mrs. Hildvig Edwardson spoke at the dedication service of Hope Mission's new facility. She described the beginnings of Hope Mission by saying, "I say we ventured, for it meant just that—but knowing the never-failing Christ, we dared to trust him, and he opened the door of service he wanted us to enter."

As always, the ministry of Hope Mission is an adventure in serving Jesus Christ by serving people in need.

Almeda Hoath was a child when Hope Mission opened its doors. She wrote to tell us why she has "a soft spot" in her heart for Hope Mission:

> My dad had been a successful insurance salesman for London Life, but when the Depression hit no one had money to buy insurance and he was laid off. We moved from Climax, Saskatchewan, to Calgary. But there was no work there either.
>
> So my dad loaded the family into our old Willis, and we headed for Peace River. We got about four miles north of Gunn. On those wagon-track roads, the car tires had simply worn out. Dad wrapped gunnysacks around the wheels to carry on a bit farther.
>
> We stopped in front of a farm. The family came out, and they invited us in for supper. I knew

my dress was dirty, and that worried me. But I forgot about that when, for the first time in my life, I ate wild blueberry pie! After supper they told us that we could stay in a small empty granary until we figured out what to do.

Bill Scott, our new friend, told my dad that he should homestead right around there. Dad was able to get 10 dollars, and he filed on the homestead. We had to chop down bush and trees in front of the car until we got to the spot where our new home would be. Bill had an old sawmill and some tools, and he helped us build a log shack. Other neighbours brought us vegetables, and we picked wild fruit that Mom canned.

But when winter came we were so short of clothes that we were in danger of freezing. Then, somehow, we got a "care package" from Hope Mission. It was a big box of winter clothes and shoes and moccasins. What a blessing! And I will never forget that in the box was also a jigsaw puzzle. It was a picture of a group of RCMP in the red uniforms. My brothers and I never had any toys, and we put that puzzle together hundreds of times. We survived thanks to Hope Mission, and so did a lot of others in those hard times. God bless the Hope Mission!

As the Mission and its supporters look to the future, it is helpful to recall the stories that built the Mission, the stories that *grew hope*. In these stories we remember and see the faith and commitment to a calling. In the decisions that mattered, the leadership of the Mission moved in faith. So often the dreams that spawned those very decisions were not realized until years, even decades, later. Keeping this in mind, Hope Mission is confident that God will use it in even greater ways, through others who come to serve in faith, humility and love.

Afterword

Their postures range from aggressive to fearful, from comic to tragic, defiant to defenceless. Time is a betrayer; aging rushes ahead of its natural course. Layered, worn clothes show the distance from the last point of refuge. The weather is a moody friend. Their music is tires on concrete, early morning sirens, funnelled wind. Their art is spray paint on cinder. Sweet, clinical, acrid and assaulting odours co-mingle in the air. This is life on the street; this is sad human drama. For every human there is a history. For every face there is a story.

The accumulation of our joys and sorrows are soft-sculpted into our faces. The nuances and the potencies of every experience are etched in. By dint of time, our faces—those unfinished paintings through which we meet the world—reveal the passages of our lives. While we often mask, hide or make them up, on inspection they tell our story. They are our vulnerable veneers.

But the veneers of people on the street are far more vulnerable, their faces often etched with desolation and sorrow. Their stories, the details of which are all unique and varied, beg some tragic questions.

Clearly their personal dramas have to do with deep and complex ruptures, ones that have increased in scope and number even while our living standard has steadily risen.

Whatever our image of the street person has been, the contemporary picture is far more varied. The spectrum of homeless people has been widening for the past few decades. More women and children, more youth, and more formerly institutionalized people from a greater variety of backgrounds are populating our inner city. Single unemployable and employable men and women, low income families, alcoholics, drug addicts, persons with psychiatric histories, immigrants, native Canadians, youth, disabled people, ex-offenders and the elderly make up our indigent community.

These are our "street people." While their stories are varied, what they do have in common is that they are without homes, and homelessness is almost always accompanied by a desperate sense of isolation.

Why are they there? Why did they end up on the street? First of all, the romantic notion of street life must be cleared up. The idea of the happy transient, cut loose from all responsibility, carefree and preferring life on the street, is far removed from reality. Living on the street is never a true choice. Even priviledged urban youth who chose to look for a subculture adventure, find that it quickly turns sour, with the street and its dead ends finally dictating the rules.

The real reasons for their presence are numerous and as varied and complex as the people themselves. A teenage girl told us, "When my mom found out that my stepdad was sexually abusing me, she kicked me out...I went downtown and met a girl who showed me how to turn tricks." One man said, "An industrial accident burned my feet so I couldn't work again." Or this stark recollection of a man released onto the streets after living in institutions for twenty years: "I was scared. I couldn't sleep. I didn't know nobody." Beyond this there are families that may be only one paycheque away from the street. In effect, the street is a catch-all for the outcasts of society.

For the young, a primary reason for being on the street is an intolerable home life. They are the runaways and throwaways, caught up in various forms of abuse or shuffled from house to house. They see street life as a much better alternative. For the disabled, both mentally and physically, a common factor for lack of shelter is being discharged from an institution with no prearranged place to go; another is simply discrimination in obtaining shelter. Ex-offenders also fall into this category. It is difficult to find employment with a criminal history, and it becomes easy to fall back into old patterns of substance abuse and crime. The reasons for homelessness among immigrants and refugees can be a combination of discrimination, breakdown of support or sponsorship, possible language barriers, and ineligibility for social assistance.

The increasing number of homeless First Nation's people poses a special problem. Tired of an abject life on their reservations, many drift into the city with expectations that exceed reality. The competition for employment, the discrimination, the lure of the "good life," the lack of resources and the inability to adapt to a success-oriented society all contribute to the rising substance abuse, dependence on social services, and chronic street life.

While much responsive work remains to be done by the federal Indian and Northern Affairs Department and the provincial social services, a unique problem exists for the Canadian Christian mission working with aboriginals. The existence of Christian run residential schools is still historically fresh. The documented sexual and physical abuse, not to mention the forced assimilation through the rending of children from their parents, is a cultural disaster that will take many generations to heal. Any approach outside of a humble willingness to understand historical grievances and receptivity for reconciliation will not only fail but also insult First Nation's people and perpetuate the festering existence of this cultural crime.

Among the most vulnerable people concerned with the loss of shelter are the elderly. Compounded or brought on by age are mental and physical challenges to simple survival that can sometimes be overwhelming. In the event of dwindling family and community support, an elderly person who was in the past a low wage earner or a homemaker can easily suffer the trauma of slowly slipping toward homelessness.

Inexorably tied up in the desperation of the street is that many of its tenants are dependent on drugs or alcohol. The search for the next period of semi-consciousness becomes all consuming, an endless downward spiral often leading to mental breakdown. It is disheartening to observe the incredible grip that intoxicants have upon many "street people."

Reasons for Homelessness

- lack of emotional or financial support
- deinstitutionalization
- lack of education and employment
- chronic illness and mental, behavioural and physical handicaps
- abuse in the home
- discrimination
- substance abuse

Poverty is the common denominator. In Edmonton alone, based on a count by the Edmonton Coalition on Homelessness, carried out in October 2008, there are just over 3,000 homeless and sheltered homeless. This does not take into account the thousands living in overcrowded substandard units.

How do we begin to help? We begin by listening. Michael Christensen, once a helper of Mother Teresa's, wrote, "Mother Teresa has spent a lifetime witnessing to the truth that we love God by loving God's poor." He went on to say that we need to get to know the poor, and then begin to give. Truly, we cannot help those we feel repulsed by. We need a new attitude, a new heart.